The Sources of Economic Growth in Ethiopia 1961-2009

Mulugeta Tesfay Teferi

The Sources of Economic Growth in Ethiopia 1961-2009

An Econometric Approach to Long Run Growth Analysis

LAP LAMBERT Academic Publishing

Impressum / Imprint
Bibliografische Information der Deutschen Nationalbibliothek: Die Deutsche Nationalbibliothek verzeichnet diese Publikation in der Deutschen Nationalbibliografie; detaillierte bibliografische Daten sind im Internet über http://dnb.d-nb.de abrufbar.
Alle in diesem Buch genannten Marken und Produktnamen unterliegen warenzeichen-, marken- oder patentrechtlichem Schutz bzw. sind Warenzeichen oder eingetragene Warenzeichen der jeweiligen Inhaber. Die Wiedergabe von Marken, Produktnamen, Gebrauchsnamen, Handelsnamen, Warenbezeichnungen u.s.w. in diesem Werk berechtigt auch ohne besondere Kennzeichnung nicht zu der Annahme, dass solche Namen im Sinne der Warenzeichen- und Markenschutzgesetzgebung als frei zu betrachten wären und daher von jedermann benutzt werden dürften.

Bibliographic information published by the Deutsche Nationalbibliothek: The Deutsche Nationalbibliothek lists this publication in the Deutsche Nationalbibliografie; detailed bibliographic data are available in the Internet at http://dnb.d-nb.de.
Any brand names and product names mentioned in this book are subject to trademark, brand or patent protection and are trademarks or registered trademarks of their respective holders. The use of brand names, product names, common names, trade names, product descriptions etc. even without a particular marking in this works is in no way to be construed to mean that such names may be regarded as unrestricted in respect of trademark and brand protection legislation and could thus be used by anyone.

Coverbild / Cover image: www.ingimage.com

Verlag / Publisher:
LAP LAMBERT Academic Publishing
ist ein Imprint der / is a trademark of
OmniScriptum GmbH & Co. KG
Heinrich-Böcking-Str. 6-8, 66121 Saarbrücken, Deutschland / Germany
Email: info@lap-publishing.com

Herstellung: siehe letzte Seite /
Printed at: see last page
ISBN: 978-3-659-46973-2

"THE ANALYSIS OF THE SOURCES OF ECONOMIC GROWTH IN ETHIOPIA"

1961-2009

An Econometric Approach Based Growth Accounting

BY: MULUGETA TESFAY: MSc IN DEVELOPMENT ECONOMICS

JUNE, 2011

1

ACKNOWLEDGMENT

I express my profound thanks to almighty GOD who granted me courage, determination and potential to undertake and accomplish this research work. I feel great pleasure in extending my sincere gratitude to Dr. Dawit Alemu. He provided me his scholarly and adept advice for improving the stuff contained in this work. He exercised great patience in examining and improving the draft of this thesis. It is due to his kind help that this paper took the present form. I once again express my heartily thanks and wish the best of his health and his services for the nation and the noble profession (Economics).

I am also thankful to my dearest brothers Tsegaye G/kidan and Berhanu Girmay for their valuable suggestions, encouragement and financial supports. My Mom Desta deserves special thanks for her unprecedented efforts she made in bringing me up. She faced all the hardships in this regard with a smiling face and kept on praying for me. For all the good attributes of this work the credit goes to the above listed personalities. May GOD consecrate the destitute!

TABLE OF CONTENTS

Contents   **pages**

4

LIST OF TABLES AND FIGURES

LIST OF ACRONYMS

CD	Cobb-Douglas
CES	Constant Elasticity of Substitution
CSA	Central Statistical Agency
EERPI	Ethiopian Economic policy and Research Institute
EPRDF	Ethiopian People Revolutionary Democratic Front
FAO	Food and Agricultural Organization
GDP	Gross Domestic Product
GFCF	Gross Fixed Capital Formation
GNP	Gross National Product
IMF	International Monetary Fund
MDG	Millennium Development Goals
MoFED	Ministry of Finance and Economic Development
NIE	Newly Industrialized Economies
R & D	Research and Development
TFP	Total Factor productivity
UNDP	United Nation Development Program
WB	World Bank

ABSTRACT

The study is focused to point out sources of economic growth in Ethiopia covering the period from 1961 to 2009. For this purpose, the study utilized the econometric model based growth accounting exercise to obtain the reliable estimates of the contribution of labor, capital and total factor productivity. The empirical evidence indicates that accumulation of physical capital is dominant in explaining the positive growth record over the last five decades accounting for more than half of the growth in output. Its role is the highest during the imperial and the EPRDF regimes where massive investment in infrastructure and social services had been undertaken. The contribution of labor is also found to be considerable with a share averaging 38 percent of the growth in GDP over the stated period. The share of total factor productivity in economic growth however has been negligible constituting only 4.5 percent of the overall growth during that period. Even worse, total factor productivity was negative during the entire Derg period. The period between 2004 and 2009 witnessed higher improvements in productivity. On the basis of these empirical findings, it may be proposed that an economic policy focused on the promotion of public and private investment on physical capital could further enhance economic growth. Along with this, investments to augment the quality and employment of labor are also vital sources of growth. Furthermore, more openness, political stability and higher investment to GDP ratio are related to better factor productivity.

7

CHAPTER-ONE

INTRODUCTION

1.1. Background

Ethiopia is a land locked country located in the eastern horn of Africa with a total surface area of 1,127,127 km^2 .With a population of over 73 million in 2007; it is the second most populous country in Africa (CSA, 2008). The history of human evolution regards Ethiopia as the origin of human beings. Its history as a political entity stretches back to antiquity, and almost uniquely within Sub-Saharan Africa, it has never been colonized.

Located near the tropics, Ethiopia hosts diverse topography ranging from the lowest (125 m below sea level) to the highest (4,533m above sea level). This has resulted in diverse ecological zones with deserts in the Eastern lowlands, to rain forests in the South-West with a great deal of endemic species. Three climatic zones - the cool, temperate and hot zone can be found within Ethiopia. The country is endowed with abundant natural resources making it among the top 5 African countries with key agriculture related natural resources.

The economy heavily relies on agriculture for income, employment and foreign exchange generation. As per the 2007/08 GDP statistics, agriculture contributed 44.6% to GDP and employed almost 85% of the labor force; the shares of service and industrial sectors being 43.5% and 11.9% respectively. Agriculture accounted for 80% of the 2 billion export earnings obtained in 2009. The main exportable agricultural products are Coffee, pulses, oils seeds & spices, Chat and Horticulture produces. The agricultural sector depends on fluctuating rainfall and poor cultivation practices and has suffered numerous catastrophic droughts.

Economic performance in Ethiopia is highly correlated with conflict and political processes. The last four decades have witnessed a cyclic evolution of policy and growth regimes. The period since 1960 can be broken down readily into the Imperial (1930-1974), Derg (1974-1991) and EPRDF (since 1991) sub-periods. The Imperial Regime pursued a market based economic policy and attempted to modernize the country through the expansion of social and infrastructure services. GDP growth averaged 4 percent over the final phase (1960-1974) of the imperial rule

8

average per capita growth being roughly 1.5 %. A large proportion of such growth was attributed to capital accumulation via huge investment in infrastructure (Alemayehu et.al, 2005).

With the market repressive and collectivist economic system of the Derg, Growth decelerated to 2.3 percent (-0.4 percent in per capita terms). Growth highly depended on Agriculture and hence was uneven due its vulnerability to the vagaries of nature. The growth share of capital and factor efficiency was very weak and negative respectively. The large investment on education led to a better role of education per worker (Alemayehu, 2003a).

The structural adjustment policies of EPRDF led to quite impressive growth records during 1990/91-1999/00. Real total and per-capita GDP grew at average rates of 3.7% and 0.7% percent per annum respectively. The contribution of capital and factor productivity to growth was strong in the late 1990s. Furthermore, the economy has registered a consecutive 6-year double digit growth for the period 2004-2009. And the output growth was relatively broad based and less volatile with the three main sectors each not falling below 6% growth (MoFED, 2009).

Yet Ethiopia remains one of the developing countries with lower measures of overall development indicators. Per capita GDP in the year 2009 approximated $ 779 at PPP (UNDP, 2009). The percentage of population earning below 1 dollar a day approximated 23 % during 1990-2004(UNDP, 2006). The poor social services are indicated by the high child, maternal and illiteracy rates of (126.8/1, 000), (871/100,000) respectively. The infrastructural development is inadequate with only 2,358 electricity connected towns, a road network of 44,359 km, and only 2 million mobile telephone subscribers by 2007(MoFED, 2009).

1.2.   Statement of the Problem

Achievement of sustained output growth has become one of the fundamental objectives of development economics and macroeconomic policy. Researchers and policy makers consider it essential, though not sufficient, for raising standards of living. Thus, study of the determinants of output growth has become preoccupation of many economists (Ahmed, 2007).

Sustained economic growth has especially been more essential for developing economies suffering from a variety of social and economic troubles. Although many observers over the last half century identified Ethiopia as a land of great potential with intelligent and industrious people, Ethiopia has had one of the lowest growth rates in the world over the past half-century and as a result remains one of the least developed nations in the world (Easterly, 2006). Generalized and chronic poverty, low income and productivity, sluggish and unsustainable growth process, widespread unemployment, major disasters of drought and famine and widespread social and economic evils characterized the economy for several years.

In particular, Output growth averaged 4 percent during the imperial era which later appallingly slowed down to 2.3 percent (-0.4 percent in per capita terms) during the military regime (Alemayehu et al, 2005).The per capita GDP measure remained inert and very low close to US \$120 until 2004 after which it started to improve. The Human Development Index measure of overall economic and social progress rates Ethiopia among the bottom (171th out of 177 countries in 2009 with HDI value of 0.41 which is lower than the average for sub-Saharan Africa). Close to 44.2 % of the population lives below the national poverty line and the average Ethiopian is expected to live 56.1 years (UNDP, 2009). Some 4.9 million people were reported to be at risk of food insecurity As of January 2009 by the government of Ethiopia. External borrowing and debt as a percentage of GDP approximated 2.8 and 13.3 respectively for 2007/08(MoFED, 2009).

However, Ethiopia has registered rapid growth since the current reformist regime took power. Real GDP growth averaged 4.0 percent during 1991/92-2003/04. According to government statistics, the fiscal year ending June 2009 marked the sixth consecutive year of double-digit GDP growth rate. Real GDP has grown by 11.05, on average, between 2003/04 and 2008/09. Growth in industrial and services sectors went up from 5.1 percent and 5.2 percent in 2000/01 to

10.4 percent and 17 percent in 2007/08 respectively. Despite its fluctuation, agricultural sector growth averaged 6.9 percent for 2000-2008 (MoFED, 2009).

The growth was not just higher now but also broader-based and less volatile that the three main economic sectors grew strong (each at least 6 percent) and more than Sixty percent of the 18 sub-categories of the national income statistics registered 8 percent growth for the period 2004-2008. Moreover, the human development report for 2010 puts Ethiopia at the "top movers" developing countries with dramatic progress in health, education and basic living standards. It reports that life expectancy at birth increased by almost 5 years, gross national income per capita rose up by 75 per cent and expected years of schooling improved by 4 years between 2000 and 2009. Such growth period is however intact with very weak per capita measures, macroeconomic imbalances and food security problems.

Comprehensive empirical studies about the long-run growth process in Ethiopia (such as easterly (2006) Alemayehu et al (2005), Alemayehu et al (2008) and Netsanet (1997) have attempted to analyze the growth process and identify the components of output growth in Ethiopia for the four decades since 1960. The growth record in the recent decade remains to be incorporated and examined under the long run growth frame work. Examining the growth process in the last five decades and indentifying its sources helps to evaluate past performance and understand the future viable economic policy measures to further sustain economic growth and enhance welfare of the society. Accordingly, this study will attempt to analyze the growth record and unravel the factors that contributed to aggregate output changes and total factor productivity growth by including the recent growth periods.

1.3.   Objectives of the Study

The present study generally intends to assess the sources of aggregate output growth in Ethiopia over the period 1961-2009. Moreover, the paper attempts to achieve the below listed specific objectives:

- survey the overall performance of Ethiopia's economy since 1960
- Examine the sources of growth in Ethiopia and assess the empirical relationship between economic growth, and the growth of labor and capital inputs and total factor productivity.
- Propose relevant policy measures based on the findings obtainable.

1.4.   Significance of the Study

The successful completion of this study is expected to serve various purposes. First, individuals intending to undertake further investigation on the issue would find it a useful supplementary material. Second, the findings would assist policy makers in evaluating past interventions and designing potential policy measures to further promote economic growth. Third, the research output is supposed to augment to and consolidate the existing of body theoretical and empirical knowledge on growth. Finally, any reader interested to learn about the pattern of growth in Ethiopia would gain a lot from this exhaustive discussion of the Ethiopian economy.

1.5.   Scope and Limitation of the Study

The study has been confined to examining the pattern of growth and identifying the sources of aggregate output and total factor productivity growth pertaining to the period 1961-2009.

With regard to limitation, data about output and labor and capital inputs is not available prior to 1961. Thus empirical analysis about the imperial regime has been constrained to the final 14 years of its rule. Likewise, capital input is not available in the national income accounts and is rather estimated from the gross fixed capital formation data reflecting measurement errors related capital formation in national income statistics to affect capital stock estimation. In the same way, it is difficult to obtain consistent data on these macro variables from different publications. Lastly, no adequate financial resource was available to conduct the study but courage.

1.6. Organization of the Paper

The paper is structured in such a manner that the first chapter introduces the entire work while the second chapter reviews theoretical and empirical literature relevant to the study. Likewise, the third part gives a survey of the political economy setting and the performance of the Ethiopian economy for the last five decades. The fourth one provides the descriptions for the nature and sources of data and methodology utilized; and makes a detailed empirical analysis of the growth process during the period 1961-2009. Finally, the fifth chapter concludes the main elements of the empirical findings and presents the respective policy proposals forwarded.

CHAPTER –TWO

LITERATURE REVIEW

2.1. Theoretical Literature Review

2.1.1. Definition of concepts

Economic Growth: Economic growth is often defined as the Quantitative change or expansion in a country's economy. Economic growth is conventionally measured as the percentage increase in real Gross Domestic Product (GDP) or Gross National Product (GNP) during one year. Growth can be nominal which includes inflation or real that growth adjusted for inflation. Economies can either grow "extensively" by using more resources (such as physical, human, or natural-capital) or "intensively" by using the same amount of resources more efficiently (productively).

Economic growth plays a decisive role to improve society's welfare. Yet it may not necessarily feed in to economic development unless GDP per capita (income distribution) improves. The impact of output growth on the real living standards of the people depends on whether growth rate of GDP exceeds population growth rate or not. Per capita GDP growth rate indicates the actual increase in average income being experienced by the people of the country. Hence, Per capita income growth is still only a component of the broad concept of economic development that requires economic, political, social, cultural and institutional transformations.

Total Factor Productivity Growth: growth of total factor productivity can be defined as the change in output holding measured inputs constant or net of the growth of measured inputs. It represents the improvements in the production technology accruing from the growth in the stock of unmeasured intangible investments such as human and R&D capital, advertising, good will, market development, information system, software, business methods, land, natural resource, water resources, the environment, and genuine technical and allocative efficiency. It also reflects the way in which technological innovation allows capital and labor to be used in more effective and valuable ways. It is also called as 'measure of ignorance' of the effects of all other range of variables not included to output growth. Total factor productivity growth is usually measured as a "residual" or as the effect of a time trend variable.

2.1.2. Economic Growth Theories

Economic growth is the primary source of the welfare of societies and hence one of the vital subjects in economic theory. The discipline of economics, for several centuries, has been trying to understand the mechanism of welfare generation and to propose suitable policy proposals. In particular, the study of the determinants of economic growth has attracted growing attention in both theoretical and applied research over the last three decades. Nevertheless, a generalized or unifying theory that elucidates the process underlying the process of economic performance is still lacking.

Despite the absence of a single all-inclusive theory, there are several partial theories that discuss the role of various factors in determining economic growth. Two main strands - the neoclassical, based on the Solow's growth model, that emphasize investment and the more recent new growth theories diverting attention to human capital and innovation capacity- can be distinguished. Moreover, Myrdal's cumulative causation theory, the New Economic Geography School and other explanations emphasizing the role of non-economic factors have had vital contributions to economic growth theory. This section will discuss the two major strands of growth theory in more detail and touch on other non- economic explanations on the growth process.

2.1.2.1. Classical growth theory

Studies about the problem of economic growth go as far back as economics was recognized as a distinct discipline. The modern conception of economic growth began with the critique of Mercantilism, especially by the phsiocrats and with the Scottish Enlightenment thinkers such as David Hume and Adam Smith. The theory of the physiocrats was that productive capacity, itself, allowed for growth and the improving and increasing capital to allow that capacity was "the wealth of nations". They stressed the importance of agriculture and saw urban industry as "sterile". In contrast, Adam Smith (1776) extended the notion that manufacturing was central to the entire economy and proposed that increasing returns and externalities out of increased division of labor along with free market would spur development. David Ricardo (1851) emphasized investment in machinery to achieving economic growth. His theory of "comparative advantage" considered the benefit from trade as an essential component of growth. Karl Marx (1867) also saw investment in machinery and capital accumulation as major sources of growth.

John Stuart Mill (1900) instead highlighted education and the sciences as engines of growth (Greiner et al, 2005)

All the classical authors stated that free market economic activity must be complemented by social and public infrastructure. Besides, the classical economists suggested that the development of market forces and economic growth would go with inequality. Economic expansion alters production methods, sectoral composition and required skills leaving income of some groups depressed while other agents accumulate fortunes. Particularly, Schumpeter (1935) conceived economic growth as a process of "creative destruction" making some gainers and others losers. Furthermore, they perceived growth as a process that converges in the long run toward a stationary state level of per capita income.

In the modern period, after Keynes's theory of aggregate demand (1936) that focused more rather on the role of aggregate consumption and investment demand as the driving force for economic growth, growth theory was furthered by the seminal contributions of Harrod (1939, 1948), Domar (1946, 1957) and then of Solow (1956, 1957) and Swan (1956) and of Kaldor (1956, 1961, 1966).

2.1.2.2. The Neoclassical Growth Model

The notion of growth as increased stocks of capital goods further developed in the 1950s. The neoclassical growth model developed by Solow (1956) and Swan (1956) propose that a sustained positive growth rate of output per capita goes beyond capital accumulation and is attained only through continual advances in technological knowledge. The effects of diminishing returns would eventually cause economic growth to cease in the absence of technological progress. This neoclassical growth model, discussed in detail below, is the starting point to modeling long-run growth analytically.

i.   Specification and Assumptions

The Solow model emphasizes four variables: namely output (Y), capital (K), labor (L) and "knowledge" or "the effectiveness of labor" (A). The economy has certain amounts of capital, labor and knowledge combined to produce output. The production function takes the form:

$$Y(t) = F(K(t), A(t)L(t)) , \qquad (2.1)$$

16

Where t denotes time.

Time does not enter the production function directly but only through K, L and A to show that output changes over time only if the inputs to production change. Specifically, the aggregate supply of output from given quantities of labor, capital and technological progress grows over time.

Note also that A and L enter the production function multiplicatively. AL is referred to as effective labor and technological progress that enters in this fashion is known as labor augmenting or Harrod neutral. The way technological progress is specified along with other assumptions imply that the capital output ratio ultimately settles down.

The central assumptions of the model concern the properties of the production function and the evolution of the three inputs in to the production overtime. The models critical assumption concerning production function is that it has constant returns to scale in its two arguments, capital and effective labor that doubling the quantities of capital and effective worker doubles the amount produced. More generally, multiplying the arguments by any non negative constant c causes output to change by the same factor. That is:

$$F(cK, cAL) = cF(K, AL) \quad \text{For all } c \geq 0 \qquad (2.2)$$

The assumption of constant returns to scale emanates from the premises that the economy is big enough that the gains from specialization has been exhausted as well as inputs other than capital, labor and knowledge does not appear to be the major constraints to growth. The good reason in assuming constant returns to scale in the Solow model lies in fact that it allows to intensively working with the production function. Setting $c = 1/AL$ in equation above yields:

$$F\left(\frac{K}{AL}, 1\right) = \frac{1}{AL} F(K, AL) \qquad (2.3)$$

Where K/AL is the amount of capital per unit of effective worker, and $F(K, AL)/AL$ is Y/AL that is output per unit of effective worker. Define $k = K/AL$, $y = Y/AL$ and $f(k) = F(K, 1)$, then we can rewrite equation (2.3) as:

$$y = f(k) \qquad (2.4)$$

17

Hence, output per unit of effective labor depends only on quantity of capital per unit of effective worker but not on the overall size of the economy (stock of capital). This intensive form production function is assumed to satisfy $f(0) = 0, f'(k) > 0, f''(k) < 0$, $\lim_{k \to 0} f'(k) = \infty$ and $\lim_{k \to \infty} f'(k) = 0$. This can be stated as no output may be expected in the absence the inputs; and the marginal product of capital is positive but declines as capital rises respectively. Likewise, the role of the two conditions is to ensure that the path of the economy does not diverge.

The other assumption relates to how the stocks of labor, capital and knowledge change over time. Labor and knowledge are assumed to grow at constant exogenous rates of n and A and thus:

$$dL(t)/dt = nL(t) \quad \text{And } dA(t)/dt = gA(t) \tag{2.5}$$

Applying the fact that the growth rate of a variable equals the rate of change of its log and relating it to equation 2.5, the labor and technological progress are assumed to grow exponentially as in equation 2.7 below:

$$\ln(L(t)) = \ln(lL) + nt \text{ And } \ln(A(t)) = \ln A_0 + gt \tag{2.6}$$

$$L(t) = L_0 e^{nt} \text{ And } A(t) = A_0 e^{gt} \tag{2.7}$$

Similarly, output is divided between consumption and investment and the fraction of output devoted to investment, s is supposed to be exogenous and constant, and existing capital depreciates at a rate δ. Thus

$$dK(t)/dt = sY(t) - \delta K(t) \tag{2.8}$$

ii.   The Dynamics of the Model

Since labor and knowledge are assumed exogenous, analyzing the behavior of the stock of capital characterizes the economy. Besides, because the economy may be growing over time, it turns out to be much easier to focus on capital stock per unit of effective labor, k, than on the unadjusted capital stock K. Since $k = K/AL$, then the chain rule can be used to drive the rate of change of capital stock per effective labor:

$$\frac{dk(t)}{dt} = \frac{dK(t)/dt}{A(t)L(t)} - \frac{K(t)}{\left[A(t)L(t)\right]^2}\left[A(t)dL(t)/dt + L(t)dA(t)/dt\right]$$

$$\frac{dk(t)}{d(t)} = \frac{dK(t)/dt}{A(t)L(t)} - \frac{K(t)}{A(t)L(t)}\frac{dL(t)/dt}{L(t)} - \frac{dA(t)/dt}{A(t)} \tag{2.9}$$

Substituting $dk(t)/dt = sY(t) - \delta k(t)$, $dL(t)/dt) = n$, $dA(t)/dt = g$, in the above yields:

$$\frac{dk(t)}{dt} = \frac{sY(t) - \delta K(t)}{A(t)L(t)} - k(t)n - k(t)g \tag{2.10}$$

Finally using the fact that $Y/AL = f(k)$, we have

$$\frac{dk(t)}{dt} = sf(k) - (\delta + n + g)k(t) \tag{2.11}$$

The above key equation of the Solow model states that the rate of change of capital stock per unit of effective labor is the difference between the actual investment per unit of effective labor $(sf(k)$ and the break even investment required to keep k at its existing level $(\delta + n + g)k(t)$ by offsetting the effects of depreciation and changes in the effective labor. Therefore, when actual investment per unit of effective labor exceeds break even investment, capital stock per effective labor rises. When actual investment falls short of breakeven investment, capital stock per unit of effective labor falls and it is constant when the two are equal.

When capital stock per effective labor converges to its maximum level (k^*), the capital stock grows at $n + g$ and constant returns to scale implies that output grows at $n + g$. Finally, capital per worker and output per worker grow at a rate of g. Thus, the Solow model implies that the economy converges to a balanced growth path where each variable grows at a constant rate and the growth rate of output per worker solely to be determined by the stock of capital per worker.

However, changes in rate of saving may affect the economy on the balanced growth path. The increase in saving rate raises the actual investment above the break even investment until it reaches a new value of k^*, at which it remains constant. The level of output per worker then grows at the level of both A and k (because $Y/L = Af(k)$) until the new k^* is attained after which it rises at g. The increase in savings rate produces a temporary increase in the growth rate of output per worker. Thus a change in the saving rate has a level effect but not a growth effect in that it changes the economy's balanced growth path and level of output but does not affect the growth rate of output per worker on the balanced growth path.

In sum, the neoclassical growth model makes two predictions. First, it identifies differences in capital per worker and in effectiveness of labor as the likely sources of variation in output per worker either over time or across parts of the world. The second important prediction concerns the notion of convergence-a process by which economies with low starting values of per capita output (poor countries) grow faster than those with higher initial values (rich countries) and the level of per capita output in all countries will converge to a common level.

Convergence occurs in the neoclassical model because of at least three reasons. First, the Solow model predicts countries converge to their balanced growth paths and thus to the extent the differences in output per worker arise from countries at different points relative to their growth paths one would expect poor countries to catch up with the rich ones. Second, the Solow model implies that the rate of return on capital is lower in countries with more capital per worker that create incentives for capital to flow from rich to poor countries causing convergence. Finally, if there are lags in the diffusion of knowledge, income difference can arise because some countries are not yet allowing the best available technologies and these gaps may tend to shrink as poorer countries gain access to the state-of-art methods.

2.1.2.3. New Growth Theory

New Growth Theory is a view of the economy that regards technological progress as a product of economic activity which Previous theories treated it as a given, or a product of non-market forces. New Growth Theory is often called "endogenous" growth theory in that it internalizes technology into a model of how markets function. It emphasizes that sustained economic growth results from the increasing returns associated with new knowledge (Petrakos et al 2007).

The endogenous growth model attempts to internalize technological change based on the presumption that innovation is both a non-rival and partially excludable public good. Non-rival implies use many times simultaneously in the production processes without restricting others from using it while partial excludability relates to the innovator's right to take the benefit of using this new innovation at the first stage. The market power by some firms, restriction mechanisms such as patents, property rights and copy rights, and the time lag of the innovator indicate elements of partial control and opportunity to make profits.

The model also assumes increasing returns to scale and imperfect market structures from the spillover effect of knowledge and the monopolistic competition between firms. Hence, these different assumptions of the endogenous growth models result in different socially optimal growth paths and have different policy implications from that of the neoclassical growth theories.

There are numerous theoretical studies that belong to endogenous growth theory in that these models construct the framework of endogenous growth theory by analyzing different dimensions of the growth process such as externalities, returns to scale, market structure, equilibrium and optimal growth rate, etc. However, the theoretical framework of endogenous growth theory can be divided into two types. In the first type, there are models of invention [Romer (1990a), Grossman and Helpman (1991a, 1991b), Aghion and Howitt (1992), Segerstrom et al. (1990), Segerstrom (1998b)], which emphasize on research activities. In the second type, there are models of learning-by-doing [Lucas (1988), Stokey (1988, 1991)] focusing on product variety.

The new growth theory started with Romer's 1986 paper which explains persistent economic growth by referring to the role of externalities. Externalities, arising from learning by doing and knowledge spillover, positively affect the productivity of labor on the aggregate economy. Likewise, Lucas (1988) and Stokey (1988) stresses the creation of human capital while Romer (1990), Grossmann and Helpman (1991) and Aghion and Howitt (1992)] focus on innovation as important sources of economic growth. In the Romer model, the stock of ideas is the most important while Grossman and Helpman emphasized spillover effects in the research sector to sustained per capita growth. These studies conclude that an increase in the factors of production that are used in the innovation process increases the rates of innovation and economic growth (Griener et al, 2005).

On the other hand, Jones (1995b) states that the economic growth rate of major OECD countries stagnates or declines in spite of increases in R&D expenditures. Jones (1995a), thus, proposes a new model- called the semi-endogenous R&D based model and discovers that economic growth rate in the long run only depends on exogenously determined population (or labor force) growth. Similarly, Segerstrom (1998b) states that the number of patents does not increase as much as the number of scientists and engineers engaged in R&D activities. Segerstrom finds that the long-run growth rate depends on population growth, size of innovation and the degree of difficulty (Romer,2006).

Young (1993) tries to combine the models of invention and learn by doing. He proposes inventions to determine the extent of learning by doing and thus further improvement in production techniques. Moreover, young goes on to state that the relative cost of invention and the size of the market matters. The society's cumulative learning experience is enhanced if the cost of invention is comparatively lower than the market size due to increased rate of invention and profitability.

2.1.2.4. Theory of Cumulative Causation

The growth theory of cumulative causation developed by Myrdal (1957) and Kaldor (1970), argues that initial conditions determine economic growth of places in a self-sustained and incremental way. Thus, economic inequalities among economies become evident. The growth centrifugal effects cannot stabilize the system with free interplay of market forces despite the growth spread effect from advanced to the less advanced economies unless economic policy comes into play to correct those imbalances. Unlike the others, theories of cumulative causation has a medium term view and often described as "soft" development theories due to a lack of applied mathematical rigor (Petrakos et al, 2001).

2.1.2.5. New Economic Geography

New Economic Geography asserts that economic growth tends to be an unbalance process favoring the initially advantaged economies by developing a formalized system of explanations which places explicit emphasis on the compound effects of increasing returns to scale, imperfect competition and non-zero transportation costs. This theory states that economic activity tends to agglomerate in a specific region and choose a location with a large local demand resulting in a self-reinforcing process.

The spatial distribution of economic activity can be explained by agglomeration (or centripetal) forces and dispersion (or centrifugal) forces. The former include backward and forward linkages of firms, externalities and scaled economies while the latter include negative externalities, transport costs and intensification of competition. Consequently, New Economic Geography is mainly concerned with the location of economic activity, agglomeration and specialization rather that economic growth. However, growth outcomes can be inferred from its models.

2.1.3. Approaches to Accounting for Economic Growth

There exist a number of methods for decomposing sources of growth over time and for estimating total factor productivity in the growth literature. The most widely used ones namely: The Growth Accounting Method; The Index Number Method and The Econometric Method are reviewed here. Each of these approaches is explained below for better understanding of the empirical analysis.

2.1.3.1. Growth Accounting Method

This approach utilizes the standard neoclassical production function as a starting point for decomposing the contribution of factor inputs and technological change to output growth.

$$Y = F(K, L, t) \qquad (2.12)$$

Where Y represents output, K capital input, L labor input and t for the time.

Differentiating equation (2.12) with respect to time, dividing it by Y, and rearranging it, yields

$$\frac{dY/dt}{Y} = \frac{\partial F/\partial K}{Y}\frac{dK/dt}{K} + \frac{\partial F/\partial L}{Y}\frac{dL/dt}{L} + \frac{\partial F/\partial t}{Y} \qquad (2.13)$$

The term $(\partial F/\partial t)/Y$ in the above equation represents the proportional rate of shift of the production function. It is also known as technical change or TFP. The terms $(\partial F/\partial K)/Y$ and $(\partial F/\partial L)/Y$ are the factor shares of capital and labor respectively. If we denote growth rates of output, capital and labor inputs by small letters like y, k and l and the shares of capital and labor by S_K and S_L respectively, then, equation (2.13) can be rewritten as:

$$y = S_K k + S_L l + TFPG \qquad (2.14)$$

23

Using the data for growth rates of Y, K and L and for the factor shares of K and L, equation (2.14) can be used to calculate the total factor productivity growth. Hence, TFPG is calculated as a residual. It proxies a "catch-all" variable and accounts for that part of output growth not explained by the growth of factor inputs. Besides, it measures the shift in production function which might be due to technical innovation, institutional change, change in the societal attitude, fluctuation in demand, changes in factor shares, omitted variables and measurement error. To avoid the bias due to omitted variables, human capital is included in equation (2.14) in two ways. One way is to treat human capital as one factor of production and repeating the above steps modifies equation (2.14) as:

$$y = \alpha k + \beta l + \lambda h + TFP \tag{2.15}$$

Where $\alpha + \beta + \lambda = 1$, $h = H^{\bullet}/H$ =growth of human capital and λ is its share in national income. Average years of schooling of adult population are used as proxy for human capital.

The other is to adjust the labor input for variation in labor quality as measured by wage differentials between groups of distinct education attainment. Education or training is embodied in the workers and thus better to adjust the input for variations in its quality instead of including it separately. Denoting the growth rate of adjusted labor and capital inputs by l^{*} and k^{*}, yields:

$$y = S_{K}k^{*} + S_{L}l^{*} + TFP \tag{2.16}$$

Barro (1998) suggested a dual approach to estimate sources of growth through growth accounting method using growth rates of factor price rather than growth rate of factor quantities. This approach states that a linear homogenous production function equates output to total factor income, which may be written as

$$Y = rK + wL \tag{2.17}$$

Where, w is wage rate and r is rental price of capital. Differentiating the above and dividing, on both sides, by gives

$$\frac{Y^\bullet}{Y} = \frac{1}{Y}\left[r^\bullet K + rK\right] + \frac{1}{Y}\left[w^\bullet L + wL^\bullet\right] \qquad (2.18)$$

Multiplying and dividing the first bracketed term by rK and the second by wL and rearranging yields the dual measure:

$$\frac{Y^\bullet}{Y} - S_K\left[\frac{K^\bullet}{K}\right] - S_L\left[\frac{L^\bullet}{L}\right] = TFPG = S_K\left[\frac{R^\bullet}{R}\right] + S_L\left[\frac{L^\bullet}{L}\right] \qquad (2.19)$$

This method requires rates of return on capital and wage rate which are not normally available especially in developing countries. The rate of interest may be used as proxy for rate of return on capital but biases the estimation for it is fixed by government authorities.

The growth accounting method to estimate growth sources has certain merits. First, it is very simple and easy to apply. Second, it can be applied when data is missing or scarce for some periods. Finally, it provides detail estimation for each period enabling regular monitoring of the economy. However, it also suffers from various pitfalls. One relates to the assumption of stable production function which may not be the case in the long run. Second, this method assumes linear homogeneity or constant returns to scale where as in reality there could be increasing returns to scale. Third, it assumes technological progress as hicks neutral that it increases the efficiency of labor and capital at the same rate while it may affect efficiencies of inputs differently. Fourth, this method is incapable of decomposing TFPG in to its constituent sources. Fifth, it is difficult to separately identify the factor shares of fixed or quasi-fixed labor share in GDP. Finally, the estimates of this model are not amenable for tests of significance. In sum, the growth accounting method is sensitive to the improvement in the quality of factor inputs, the share of factor inputs and the assumption related to the returns to scale; and overestimates the importance of local factors and does not measure the global impact.

2.1.3.2. Index Number Method

It is an extension and a complement of growth accounting method. This method does not necessitate the aggregate production function but selects an approximate index number. Measurement of productivity is complicated when more than one factor, say labor and capital, are used to produce more than one output, say x and y. There happens a problem of selecting the weights for each output and input to form an index. Standard forms of TFP index are:

$$A = Y / L^{\alpha} K^{\beta} \text{ And } A = Y / \alpha L + \beta K \tag{2.20}$$

Where A is TFP index, Y output index, L and K inputs, and α and β are respective weights. Two approaches are used for the selection of TFP index number. First, properties of various index numbers forms are compared with desirable properties and the one with the maximum number of desirable property is used. Second, a particular index number is linked to a particular production function. In view of its superiority over the other index number forms, the Divisia – Tornqvist index is often used (Ahmed, 2007). Divisia –Tornqvist index assumes linear homogenous trans-logarithmic function, profit maximization and perfect competition and is defined as:

$$Y_t = \prod_{i=1}^{m}(y_{it} / y_{it-1})^{1/2[R_{it} - R_{it-1}]} \text{ And } R_{it} = p_{it}y_{it} / \Sigma p_{it}y_{it} \tag{2.21}$$

Where Y_t refers to output index, y_{it} to quantity of ith output and R_{it} to share of ith output in total revenue.
Similarly, the Tornqvist input quantity index is defined:

$$I_t = \prod_{j=1}^{n}(x_{ji} / x_{ji-1})^{(1/2)}[s_{jt} + s_{jt-1}] \text{ And } s_{jt} = w_{jt}x_{jt} / \Sigma w_{jt}x_{jt} \tag{2.22}$$

Where I_t is for input quantity index, x_{jt} quantity of jth input, and s_{jt} share j^{th} input in total cost. The Tornqvist index is simply the ratio of output quantity index to input quantity index as:

$$TFP_t = Y_t / I_t \tag{2.23}$$

This method requires the factor payments to equal the marginal productivities and reliable data series for factor incomes. The merits and limitations of this approach are similar to the growth accounting method above.

2.1.3.3 Econometric Approach

The econometric approach specifies production, cost or profit functions and then estimates it with a suitable econometric tool. The Cobb-Douglas, trans-log and CES production functions are often used for the purpose of growth regressions and each of these functions is explained below.

a) The Trans-log Production Function

There exist direct and indirect ways of estimating this production function. The direct estimation with two inputs, capital and labor, can be written as

$$Y = \exp[\alpha_0 + \alpha_L \ln L + \alpha_L \ln K + \alpha_T T + 1/2\beta_{KK}(\ln K)^2 + \beta_{KL} \ln K \ln L + \beta_{KT} T \ln K + 1/2\beta_{LL}(\ln L)^2$$
$$+ \beta_{LT} T \ln L + \beta_{TT} T^2] + \varepsilon \tag{2.24}$$

Where Y, K, L and T are output, capital and labor inputs and technology respectively. This requires a large number of observations a problem in case of developing countries and presence of large number of parameters may result in multi-collinearity problem.

In the indirect method, first the cost or profit function is estimated and the duality theory is used to derive the production function. Ordinary Least squares is first used to obtain the residuals which then are employed to compute co-variances and Generalized Least Squares is applied along with restrictions on parameters. The Generalized Least Squares procedure is repeated again and again until the residuals are minimized.

b) The Cobb-Douglas Production Function

The Cobb-Douglas production function, common in growth literature, takes the form;

$$Y_t = A_t K^\alpha_t L_t^\beta \tag{2.25}$$

Where Y_t refers to output, K_t to capital, and L_t to labor each at time t. A_t Represents technology (TFP) parameter and α and β denote output elasticities with respect to capital and labor inputs. The technology parameter, A_t, grows at exponential rate λ and can be specified as

$$A_t = A_0 e^{\lambda t} \tag{2.26}$$

Substitution of the above equation in to equation (2.26) yields

$$Y_t = A_0 e^{\lambda t} K^\alpha_t L_t^\beta \tag{2.27}$$

27

Assuming variable returns to scale and taking logarithms on both sides of equation (2.27) gives

$$\ln Y_t = \ln A_0 + \lambda t + \alpha \ln K_t + \beta \ln L_t + \varepsilon_t \qquad (2.28)$$

An estimable form of equation (2.28) may take the form

$$\ln Y_t = \beta_0 + \beta_1 t + \beta_2 \ln K_t + \beta_3 \ln L_t + \varepsilon_t \qquad (2.29)$$

But under the constant returns to scale, the estimable form of equation (2.29) becomes

$$\ln Y_t / L_t = \beta_0 + \beta_1 t + \beta_2 \ln K_t / L_t + \varepsilon_t \qquad (2.30)$$

Where β_2 represents the share of capital in output and partial elasticity of value added with respect to capital. The share of labor input will be one minus the share of capital.

C. The Constant Elasticity of Substitution (CES) Production Function

The general form of the CES production can be written as:

$$Y_t = \lambda \left[\delta K_t^{-\rho} - (1-\delta) L_t^{-\rho} \right]^{\frac{v}{\rho}} e^{\varepsilon_t} \qquad (\gamma > 0, 0 < \delta < 1; v > 0; -1 \le \rho) \qquad (2.31)$$

Where γ, δ, v and ρ stand for efficiency, distribution, returns to scale and substitution parameters respectively. The constant elasticity of substitution production function includes other functions such as CD and "fixed proportions" and the substitution parameter ρ is responsible for the degree of generality. Taking natural logarithms on both sides of equation (2.31) gives us

$$\ln Y_t = \ln \gamma - v / \rho \ln \left[\delta K_t^{-\rho} + (1-\delta) L_t^{-\rho} \right] + \varepsilon_t \qquad (2.32)$$

Equation (2.32) can be linearized through the Taylor expansion process around $\rho = 0$ by dropping the terms involving powers of ρ higher than 1 and adding a time trend t to represent effect of technical change, and the estimable equation will be:

$$\ln Y_t = \beta_0 + \beta_1 t + \beta_2 \ln K_t + \beta_3 \ln L_t + \beta_4 (\ln K_t - \ln L_t)^2 + \varepsilon_t \qquad (2.33)$$

The constant elasticity of substitution δ is equal to $1/1+\rho$. The estimable form of the CD production is nested to the estimable form of the CES function and the choice of production

28

function specification between CD and CES is based on the test of the nested hypothesis. If the estimate β_4 is statistically significant, the CES is the appropriate model otherwise the CD is preferred.

As the econometric approach is based on parameter estimates, it can be subjected to statistical tests. However it requires the availability of consecutive data series for sufficiently large period and measures average contributions of factors for the entire period and does not give detailed estimates of sources of growth. This approach avoids the systematic measurement error in factor shares.

3.2.   Empirical Literature Review

Enormous differences in economic growth and levels of per capita GDP across the world's economies characterize the modern era. Some countries have grown faster and achieved high incomes while many have continued to languish in poverty. The prominent growth miracles of Japan and newly industrialized countries of East Asia since the 1960's and growth disasters of mainly sub-Saharan Africa beginning 1950's clearly highlights this fact. In sum, the world economy has grown and cross-country income differences have widened on average over the whole of the modern era. Theoretical developments about the determinants of the growth process in the last two decades have been accompanied by a growing number of empirical studies. A summary of the empirics on the growth of East Asian and sub Saharan African economies is given below.

3.2.1. Sources of growth in East Asia

East Asian developing economies as a group has, on average, grown at a rate of almost eight percent per annum since the 1960s. In contrast, the non-Asian Group-of-Five (G-5) developed economies have grown at an average rate of a little over three percent per annum. This has led some economists to consider such sustained rapid economic growth in the East Asian economies as the "East Asian miracle.

As a result, several empirical studies emphasizing on identifying the source to such rapid growth has been carried out. Studies including Tsao (1985) and Young (1992) for Singapore, Kim and Lau (1994a, 1994b) and Young (1994, 1995) for the four East Asian NIEs, Kim and Lau (1996) for extended number East Asian economies, Senhadji (1999) for the East Asian and South Asian economies, Kim and Lau (1995) for the four East Asian with extended analysis to include human capital, all provide empirical evidence in favor of the hypothesis that there has been no technological evidence(Lau and Park, 2003).

Lau and Park write that empirical findings such as Young (1992) for Hong Kong, the World Bank (1993), Collins and Bosworth (1997), Klenow and Rodriguez-Clare (1997), Sarel (1997) for the ASEAN economies, Easterly and Levine (2001), and Iwata, Khan and Murao (2002), however, provide evidence against no technical progress despite less creditability due to restrictive assumptions by some of these studies

3.2.2. Sources of growth in Sub-Saharan Africa

Growth performance in Sub Saharan Africa for the last four decades has been very weak. Growth in the region as a whole averaged 3.3 percent during 1960-2002. This barely exceeds the average population growth rate of about 3 percent and is less than half of what is needed to achieve the MDG goal of halving the number of people in absolute poverty. Only four countries (Botswana, Equatorial Guinea, The Gambia, and Mauritius) registered an average growth rate of at least 5 percent during 1960-2002 while12 countries registered an average growth of at least 5 percent during 1997-2002 (Tahari et al 2004).

The contribution of the tertiary sector (which includes public and private services) was the largest in GDP while the share of the secondary sector remained the lowest except for middle income and oil-producing countries. Likewise, GDP growth in sub Saharan Africa was driven by the tertiary sector (close to 50 percent) despite the dominance of the oil sector in oil-producing countries. The continuous deterioration in growth from the 1960s to the mid 1990s was accompanied by the large decline in the roles of agriculture and the services sectors in the 1970s, and 1980s and 1990s respectively. According to Tahari et al (2004), growth was highly correlated with the industrial (0.9) and services (0.8) sectors while it was weak for agriculture.

Rahel (2003), citing Senhadji (1999), writes that a growth accounting exercise that looked at the experience of 88 developing and developed countries indicated that sub Saharan Africa had the lowest growth during 1960 -1994 with very low total factor productivity growth. Growth was driven by accumulation in physical and human capital.

30

In the same way, Tehari et al (2004) based on literature on production function estimate for developing countries conducted growth accounting exercise for sub Saharan African countries and obtained that factor accumulation was important to growth during 1960-2000 while total factor productivity was negligible. Moreover, Physical capital constituted the dominant role to output growth. Bosworth and Collins (2003) provide a comparison of the growth performance of various sub-regions in the world during 1960-2000 and their results for sub-Saharan Africa, using a much smaller set of countries and adjusting for educational attainment, are comparable to the above findings(Tahari et al 2004). Hence, growth in sub Saharan Africa over the last 4 decades is explained by physical and human capital accumulation while the role of total factor productivity was insignificant.

3.2.3. Sources of Ethiopian past growth records

The literature on Ethiopia's long run economic growth is limited. Comprehensive empirical studies about the growth process are limited to those of Easterly (2006), Alemayehu et al (2005), Netsanet (1997), and Alemayehu et al 2008.

Easterly (2006) finds that the estimated 1.1 percent permanent component of per capita income growth rate of the Ethiopian economy in the 1992-2001 period is largely attributed to total factor productivity instead of capital deepening. He argues that growth payoff to the policy changes the government initiated, measured by inflation rate, budget deficit, and the black market premium, the ratio of M2 to GDP, level of infrastructure and the real depreciation of currency, contributed to such growth. He suggested improvements in the initial poor quality institutions, higher illiteracy, low level of openness to trade and low degree of structural transformation for further increases in the growth potential.

Alemayohu and Befekadu (2005), based on Collins and Bosworth (1996) growth accounting benchmark estimation to form a regression, have tried to decompose the source of growth for Ethiopia covering the period 1960-1997 and found that capital explains a good part the growth record (1.42 %) while the contribution of education per worker was very low (0.07%) and the total factor productivity growth was virtually negative (-0.29). They relate effect of systemic instability, shocks such as weather outturn, lack of structural change and bad polices to the fragile performance of the economy.

31

Similarly, they have estimated the share of each sector to GDP over the same period using cross-country regression approach of Chenery-Syrquin (Chenery and Syrquin 1975, Syrquin and Chenery 1989, O'Connel and Ndulu 2000) and found that although the share of each sector fluctuates in a very narrow band, it remained unchanged. Hence, Growth performance still hinges on fragile agricultural sector with no structural change in the overall economy.

Alemayohu Geda, Abebe Shimeles and John Weeks (2008) determine the sources of economic growth for Ethiopia based on a Cobb Douglas production function estimated from both macro and micro level data. The macro version of the model, using time series data on output, capital and labor for the period 1962-1998, shows the dominant role of labor in accounting for the positive growth. The average contribution of capital is negligible while that of total factor productivity is positive. In contrast, the micro based production function using a rural household survey (1500 rural households) that introduces a number of different indicates that land (size of holding) is the most significant factor that determines growth (cereal production) while labor's share was relatively lower.

Alemayehu (2008) conducted a source of growth exercise based on a model fairly close to the recent 'endogenous growth' models whose parameters are derived from cross country regression. The study examined the contribution of base variables (which include initial income/endowment, life expectancy, age dependency ratio, terms of trade shocks, trading partner growth rate and land-lockedness), political stability index (an index constructed from the average number of assassinations, revolutions and strikes) and policy indicator (high inflation rate, public spending and parallel market premium) variables contribution to the predicted deviation across the three regimes prevailed in the last four decades in Ethiopia. The base variables had the highest contribution.

Hence, different studies approached the issue of the sources of growth in Ethiopia differently and came up with varying results about the role of various components of the growth process. Micro level studies emphasize the role of land while macro level studies alternate between labor and capital.

32

CHAPTER-THREE

DATA AND RESEARCH METHODOLOGY

3.1   Description and Source of Data

Time series data about output, and labor and capital inputs covering the period 1962-2009 are required to estimate the sources of aggregate output growth in Ethiopia in this study. The proposed sample period for this study included 1960-2009. However, data about gross domestic product (GDP), economically active population and gross fixed capital formation (GFCF) is not available prior to 1961 narrowing the period to 1961-2009. Adequate data on these variables was not also available in any single publication. The data about output measured in current or real GDP obtained from MoFED, IMF, UN, and WDI failed to be identical. Hence, the MoFED data that included better details and alternative measures has been utilized.

Likewise, the data on the stock of capital is not available in the national income accounts and the Gross Fixed Capital formation measure taken from MoFED data was used to estimate it using the perpetual inventory method that determines the present stock of capital from past streams of investment. The detail of the estimation procedures for the stock of capital is given in the appendix-B of B1. The number of economically active population for Ethiopia obtained from UN data is used to measure the labor input. The measurement of labor in this study doesn't make adjustments for variations in quality of labor and hours worked as a result of improvement in education and training in the former and due to fluctuation in economic activity in the later owning to the scarcity of data on such changes for most of the study period. The annual rainfall data is taken from Ethiopian Metrology Agency data base. Data about the same variables from IMF and UN data bases has also been taken to make regressions to be used just for contrasts. GDP and capital input data are given in constant local currency unit (Birr).

3.2   Research Methodology

This study employs both the descriptive and investigative analyses to examine the growth process of the Ethiopian economy for the last five decades. The descriptive study reviews the political economy setting for growth and performance of the Ethiopian economy under the imperial, Derg and the current regimes using simple statistical techniques (averages, percentage and growth rates). On the other hand, the analytical study determines the sources of growth in Ethiopia through production function-based growth accounting exercise. The estimation methods involved in the later however need to be illustrated as follows.

3.2.1 Estimation Methods

3.2.1.1   Model specification

Understanding the sources of economic growth has been a major subject in economics as it is essential to improve standards of living. Measurement of economic growth is therefore essential in order to understand and quantify it. In the growth literature there exist a number of methods for the estimation of the sources of economic growth. Three approaches: the Growth Accounting, the Index Numbers and the Econometric approaches are the most widely used methods to accounting for output growth.

The Growth Accounting method which bases the standard neoclassical production function to split output growth in to its components basically utilizes the derived equation below:

$$y = S_K k + S_L l + TFPG \qquad (3.1)$$

Where y, k and l denote growth rates of output, and capital and labor inputs. Besides, S_K, S_L and TFP refer to, respectively, the shares of capital and labor inputs in national income accounts and total factor productivity. However, the growth accounting equation can also be formulated for growth rate of factor prices instead of factor inputs; and can be augmented /modified for improvements in human capital (Baro, 1998).

Likewise, the Index Numbers method relies on the selection of an appropriate index number for each input and output which then divides growth in to the share of inputs and TFP growth using:

$$A = Y / L^\alpha K^\beta \text{ And } A = Y / \alpha L + \beta K \qquad (3.2)$$

Where A is TFP index; Y is output index; L and K are inputs; and α and β are inputs weights.

The growth accounting and index numbers methods are often best used when national income account statistics about input shares in output are more dependable; data is missing or scarce for some periods; and detailed sectoral or periodic estimation to regularly monitor the economy is required. However, these methods are based on the restrictive assumptions of constant returns to scale and perfectly competitive markets. The estimates of such models are not also amenable to tests of significance and cannot be used to further analyze total factor productivity growth. Moreover, Analysis based on these methods in poor countries (such as Ethiopia) where national income statistics is fraught with difficulties may not be reliable. The detail of the concepts and derivations of the equations the above two equations is given in the second chapter under sub section 2.1.3.

The Econometric approach unlike the others; involves flexible assumptions with regard to returns to scale and market structure to show long run relationship between variables; avoids measurement errors related to determining the share of factor inputs in output; includes estimates that are amenable to tests of significance; and enables the split of total factor productivity growth at economy or sector level in to its constituent parts. Thus, the econometric approach that conforms to the long-period growth analysis has been utilized for this study and is explained below for better understanding of the empirical investigations.

a. The Econometric Model

The Econometric approach specifies production, cost or profit functions and then estimates it with an appropriate econometric tool. The Trans-log, Constant Elasticity of substitution and Cobb-Douglas production functions   are often used for the purpose of growth regressions. For instance, Mankiw, Romer and Weil (1992) used the CD form; Hsieh (2000) opted for the CES form while Rafaqat (1997) used the trans-log production function to study sources of growth in Pakistan (Antras, 2004). Most of the empirical studies in Ethiopia (such as Alemayehu (2008), Alemayehu et al (2005) and Easterly (2006)) used the CD production function. The specification of the production function is a crucial aspect in the estimation and analysis of sources of aggregate output growth. Specification error may result in the incorrect estimates of the share of inputs and total factor productivity growth to output growth by affecting marginal products and /or elasticities of substitution.

The estimation of the Trans-log production function involves direct and indirect approaches. The direct way of estimation is specified below (equation 4.1) while the indirect one makes use of the duality theory to derive the production function from the estimation of cost or profit functions.

$$Y = \exp[\alpha_0 + \alpha_L \ln L + \alpha_K \ln K + \alpha_T T + 1/2\beta_{KK}(\ln K)^2 + \beta_{KL} \ln K \ln L + \beta_{KT} T \ln K + 1/2\beta_{LL}(\ln L)^2$$
$$+ \beta_{LT} T \ln L + \beta_{TT} T^2] + \varepsilon \qquad (3.3)$$

Where Y, K, L and T are output, capital and labor inputs, and technology respectively. This requires a large number of observations that are rarely available in developing countries and the existence of a large number of parameters makes it susceptible to the problem of multi-collinearity. In view of the dearth of data pertaining to Ethiopia and the excess of parameters required for estimation, this production function is not considered in this study.

The estimable form of the Constant Elasticity of Substitution (CES) Production function- the derivation of which is available in the second chapter under subsection 2.1.3.3- can be reproduced as in equation 4.2 below. Following Ahmed (2007) that he adopted it from Wizarat (2004), the viability of the Constant Elasticity of Substitution (CES) Production function depends on whether the β_4 coefficient in the nested hypothesis below is significant or not. If the estimate for β_4 is statistically significant, the CES production function would be the appropriate model.

$$\ln Y_t = \beta_0 + \beta_1 t + \beta_2 \ln K_t + \beta_3 \ln L_t + \beta_4 (\ln K_t - \ln L_t)^2 + \varepsilon_t \qquad (3.4)$$

Where Y, K and L are output, and capital and labor inputs respectively. The estimation of equation 4.2 using data on output, labor and capital for the study period is provided in appendix-A of table A3. The value for the decision parameter ($\beta_4 = 0.019$) has been found to be highly statistically insignificant at any level of significance with t-statistics value of 0.64. This ensures that the Constant elasticity of Substitution production function is not the preferable specification for the growth process and has been reduced to the Cobb-Douglass production function.

36

As a result, the Econometric approach in this study specifies the basic Cobb-Douglas production function which is virtually used for estimation after certain derivations given by;

$$Y_t = A_t K_t^{\alpha} L_t^{\beta} \qquad (3.5)$$

Where Y_t, K_t and L_t represent output and capital and labor inputs at time t. In addition, A_t refers to the state of technology (Total Factor Productivity growth) and the parameters α and β are the output elasticities of capital and labor inputs respectively.

Specifying the exponential growth of technology (TFP) parameter by $A_t = A_0 e^{\lambda t}$ and substituting it in to equation (3.5) yields:

$$Y_t = A_0 e^{\lambda t} K_t^{\alpha} L_t^{\beta} \qquad (3.6)$$

Furthermore, taking logarithms on both sides of equation 3.6; and rearranging the parameters of equation 3.7 with the $\beta' s$ assuming variable returns to scale yields the estimable form of the Cob Douglas production function as in equation 3.8 below.

$$\ln Y_t = \ln A_0 + \lambda t + \alpha \ln K_t + \beta \ln L_t \qquad (3.7)$$

$$\ln Y_t = \beta_0 + \beta_1 \lambda + \beta_2 \ln K_t + \beta_3 \ln L_t + \varepsilon_t \qquad (3.8)$$

Where ε_t refers to the disturbance term. The output elasticities of capital (β_2) and labor (β_3) and the technology (TFP) coefficient of β_1 are then estimated using time series data on output, capital stock and labor (economically active population) with the help of an appropriate econometric tool. The estimation and interpretation of the CD production function is convenient because it involves only two variables particularly for poor countries where data is scarce.

The transformed Cobb-Douglas production function in equation 4.5 serves to indicate the long run (equilibrium) relationship between output and capital and labor inputs provided cointegration exists. The long run output elasticities of labor and capital inputs thus measure average (equilibrium) percentage contributions to output growth resulting from a percent change in each of these inputs over the sample period.

However, in the short run, the output elasticities of change in factor inputs may deviate from the equilibrium (long run) level. According to Gujarati (2004), if a dependent and independent variable (s) are found to be cointegrated, the Error correction model can be used to make ties between the short run behaviors of output to its long run values. Therefore, the Error Correction mechanism specified below is utilized to examine how the short run disequilibrium in output adjusts in each period.

$$\Delta \ln Y = \alpha_0 + \alpha_2 \Delta \ln K + \alpha_3 \Delta \ln L + \alpha_4 u_{t-1} + \varepsilon_t \qquad (3.9)$$

Where Δ denotes the first difference operator for the logarithm of each input, ε_t is a random error term, and $u_{t-1} = \ln Y_{t-1} - (\beta_0 + \beta_1 \lambda + \beta_2 \ln K_{t-1} + \beta_3 \ln L_{t-1})$ which is the one-period lagged value of the error term in the estimation (regression) of equation 3.8 above. The absolute value of the coefficient for the lagged disturbance term (α_4) shows how quickly the equilibrium restores.

b. The Growth Accounting Model

For the purpose of growth accounting, the estimable form of the CD production function can be further simplified by taking the first derivative of each term with respect to time on both sides of equation 3.8:

$$\frac{d \ln Y(t)}{dt} = \frac{d \ln \beta_0}{dt} + \frac{d\beta_1 t}{dt} + \frac{d\beta_2 \ln K(t)}{dt} + \frac{d\beta_3 \ln L(t)}{dt} \qquad (3.10)$$

Applying the fact that the rate of change of the logarithm of a variable equals the growth rate of that variable to equation 3.10 yields the growth accounting equation of:

$$\frac{\Delta Y}{Y} = \beta_1 + \beta_2 \frac{\Delta K}{K} + \beta_3 \frac{\Delta L}{L} \qquad (3.11)$$

Where β_2 and β_3 are the growth elasticities of capital and labor inputs and $\Delta Y / Y, \Delta K / K$ and $\Delta L / L$, respectively, are actual growth rates of output, and capital and labor inputs. The total factor productivity growth or the Solow residual ($\Delta A / A$) is then derived as residual from equation 4.8. The Solow residual proxies a "catch-all" variable and accounts for that part of output growth not explained by the growth of factor inputs.

The actual growth in output can be split in to the contribution of the growth in inputs and total factor productivity given the output elasticities and growth rates of labor and capital input with the help of equation 3.11. The contribution of an input equals the product of the output elasticity of that input and the growth rate of the same input. Growth rates for output and inputs are computed as averages for different sub periods over the sample period. The growth accounting exercise has been undertaken for the three different regimes based on both the long run and the error correction model (ECM) estimates and data on the growth rate of output, and labor capital inputs.

3.2.1.2   Diagnostic Tests

a. Unit Root Test

Empirical analysis based on time series data assumes that the underlying series is stationary. The mean, variance and auto-covariance of the stochastic process should be time invariant. Applying the standard econometric framework directly to nonstationary time series leads to the phenomenon of spurious regression where a flawed decision is made about the significance of statistical relationship between variables. The usual t-ratios are overestimated with nonsensical regression making them undependable to making tests. This may result in misleading conclusions, forecasts, and policy proposals. Hence, in dealing with time series data, the variables should be subjected to tests for stationarity before proceeding with estimation to safeguard against nonsense regression.

To this purpose, this study utilizes the unit root test which is popular test for stationarity. The Dickey and Fuller or the Augmented Dickey and Fuller (DF or ADF) tests for unit root, based on the degree of autocorrelation of the error terms, are employed to check the variables in the specified model for stationarity. The correlogram test is also undertaken to supplement the unit root test. The correlogram plots for each variable are not reported but due to the large space these plots occupy.

b. Cointegration Tests

Transformation of a non-stationary time series is required in order to run a meaningful regression. However, the problem of nonsensical regression can also be overcome by verifying if the linear combination of the variables is stationary. In other words, cointegration of the variables suffices. Even so, test for staionarity should precede cointegration tests in order to check if the variables involve the same order of integration. Only variables integrated to the order same are subjected to cointegration tests. This study takes the Engel and Granger unit root test to evaluate the existence of a stationary linear combination between output, and labor and capital inputs. This test emphasizes the stationarity of the error term from the cointegrating (long run) regression. The cointegrating regression Durbin-Watson test is also used in addition.

Besides, additional tests such as histogram normality test, white hetroschedasticity test, Breusch-Godfrey LM test for serial correlation are utilized to check the overall significance of the model. The ordinary least square method of estimation has been used to run all regressions (main and intermediate) pertaining to the econometric analysis. In addition, the user friendly (menu driven) E-views (versions there and five) software package has been utilized for estimation. Tables and graphs are used to facilitate analysis of the empirical findings.

CHAPTER- FOUR

RESULTS AND DISCUSSION

4.1   Ethiopian Economic Performance Review: Descriptive analysis

Ethiopian history has mostly been full of wars/conflict under the ideology of religion, region, nationality or a combination of these but in effect intended for power and resource control. The constant enmity between the two distinct antagonistic interest groups; the landed aristocracy to maintain their power and privileges intimately related to land; and the peasantry opposing exorbitant taxes, surplus extraction and indiscriminate plunder on one side and the fact that hostile and powerful colonial forces besieged independent Ethiopia on the other led to the development of a militaristic state with accompanying institutional set-up that is detrimental for growth. Civil wars, aggravated by wars against foreign aggressions, were the perpetual scourge of Ethiopia with the outcome of the bloodshed of combatants and depopulation, ravage of fertile land, butchering of flocks of cattle, destruction of towns and villages, and interruption of internal and external trade. This led not only to famine but also to general insecurity that deterred division of labor and productive economic activity (Alemayohu et al, 2005).

Hence, the poverty and backwardness of Ethiopia is highly correlated with conflict/wars and the political system associated with it. Frequent conflicts, drastic policy changes and reversals do adversely affect the behavior of economic agents. In conformity with such historic process, a cyclic change of policy and growth regime characterized the last five decades. Accordingly, one can readily breakdown the period beginning 1960 in to the Imperial (1930-1974), the Derg (1974-1991) and the EPRDF (since 1991) sub-periods. This section is thus devoted to describing the political economy setting and the performance of the Ethiopian economy in the three periods.

4.1.1   The Imperial Rule (1930-1974)

The imperial regime in this study refers to the reign of emperor Haileselasie I (1930-1974). The imperial government presided over essentially a feudal economy with aristocrats and the church owning most arable land and tenant farmers who paid exorbitant rents making up the majority of the nation's agriculturalists. The labor relations were largely determined by the structure of the

41

land market. The majority of rural households lived under abysmal condition. Although the imperial regime continued the historical legacy which reduced the majority of peasants to poverty, it attempted to modernize the nation through the expansion of social services, development of infrastructure, establishment and encourage establishment of import substituting industries, introduction of modern political system and formulation of medium term plans.

The general policy stance of the imperial government was to adopt the market based economic policy. The government tried to set up the institutions vital to a functioning financial and product market. It established central, commercial and development banks and capital markets; encouraged and licensed various private banks; allowed private economic activity and private ownership of land; pursued a free external trade policy and more generally liberalized the product market. However, the social and economic structure in which these institutions operated centered on the landed aristocrat.

The economic structure of the country was much as it had been for centuries when Italy evacuated in 1941 though there had been some attempts in road construction, to establish a few small industries and introduce commercial farming. During the late 1940s, the imperial regime focused its development efforts on expansion of the bureaucratic structure and ancillary services. By the 1950s, Emperor Haileselassie I pursued a new economic policy to build an agro-industrial economy through a series of centrally administered development plans. The National Economic Council (NEC) was organized to coordinate the state's development plans. This agency aimed to improve agricultural and industrial productivity, eradicate illiteracy and diseases, and improve living standards. It helped to prepare Ethiopia's first and second five-year plans.

The First Five-Year Plan (1957-61) sought to develop a strong infrastructure; set up an indigenous cadre of skilled and semiskilled personnel in processing industries; and promote commercial agricultural ventures. The Second Five-Year Plan (1962-67) aspired to diversify production, introduce modern processing methods, and expand productive capacity. The Third Five-Year Plan (1968-73), unlike the others, expressed the government's willingness to expand educational opportunities and improve peasant agriculture. The government introduced the Minimum Package Program (MPP) (1971) that include credit supply, innovative extension services, establishment of cooperatives, and provision of infrastructure mainly water supply and weather roads.

In all the three plans, growth in the whole economy and economic sectors such as agriculture, manufacturing and mining failed to meet the planned targets. For instance, during the First Five-Year Plan, gross national product grew at a 3.2 percent annual rate as opposed to the projected figure of 3.7 percent. Administrative and technical incapabilities, staffing problems in plan commissions and neglect to identify resources (personnel, equipment and funds) hindered Ethiopia's development planning.

Even so, data about selected macroeconomic indicators from MoFED (table 4.1) indicates that the economy achieved sustained economic growth during the 1960/61 to 1973/74 period. As the figures in the table below reveal, Gross Domestic product (GDP), on average, grew at 3.7 percent annually (the per capita growth being 1.3 percent) between 1960/61-1973/74. Growth in the agriculture, industrial and services sectors rose by annual averages of 2.1 percent, 6.9 percent and 7.3 percent respectively from 1960/61 to 1973/74.

Table 4.1 selected macroeconomic indicators

indicator	1960/61-1973/74	Sector	1965/66-1973/74, Average in %		
			Share in Cur. exp	Share in Cap. exp	Share in total
Real GDP growth		Economic devet	11.8	78.5	26.1
Per capita GDP	1.3	Social services	24.8	19.4	23.6
Total GDP	3.7	General service	63.4	2.1	50.3
Agriculture	2.1	Health and educ	23.1	17.9	22
Industry	6.9	capital			21.4
Services	7.3				
	1970/71-1973/74	1965/66-1973/4	sector	% Share in GDP	
	% of GDP	% change		1960/61	11973/7
Trade deficit(-)	1.6		Agriculture	75	61.7
Current accou (+)	0.2		industry	7	10.3
Overall balanc(+)	0.93		Service	17.2	28
CPI		2.96			

Source: own computations based on data from MoFED for GDP and expenditure; and the rest from EERPI (EEA) data base.

Much of the Growth in the industrial sector was driven by the growth in large and medium scale manufacturing (11.2 percent), and electricity and water works (12.5 percent) while growth in services sector was dominated by expansion of education (11.3 percent), communication and transport (9.6 percent), and banking, insurance and real estate (7.6 percent) services. Growth in these sectors is largely attributed to the massive public investment undertaken during that period. Economic and social development sectors received close to half of (49.7 percent) the government budget. Much of the capital budget was committed to transport; communication and construction works. Besides, the share of investment in GDP rose as high as close to 17 percent on average.

The economy registered a current account and overall fiscal surplus of 0.2 and 0.93 percent of GDP during the last four years of the period and average price level rose by less than 3 percent between 1965/66 and 1973/74. Relative to its neighbors, Ethiopia's economic performance was higher than Sudan's 1.3 percent rate or Somalia's 1 percent rate but lower than Kenya's 6 percent and Uganda's 5.6 percent growth rates during the same 1960/61 to 1972/73 period.

Nevertheless, these changes failed to improve the lives of most Ethiopians. About four-fifths of the population lived in poverty because they used most of their meager production to pay taxes, rents, debt payments, and bribes. Drought, tenancy and land reform problems, and lack of technological development adversely affected economic growth and livelihoods of the people.

The last fourteen years of Haileselassie's reign therefore witnessed growing opposition to his regime. The misery the system caused on the majority of the rural population; the governments alienation from all social strata; and the failure to implement laws that change the landlord-tenant relationship along with the immediate causes of government attempt to hide the famine in Northern Ethiopia, strike by taxi drivers to oil crises and strong opposition against a revised educational curriculum led to the down fall of the regime (Alemayehu et al, 2005). In early 1974, confrontation between traditional and modern forces erupted and Ethiopia entered a period of profound political, economic, and social change frequently accompanied by violence.

4.1.2 The Derg regime (1974-1991)

The Provisional Military Administrative Council (PMAC; also known as 'the Derg') assumed power in 1974 and restructured the country's political system and economic structure along the socialist lines. The economic restructuring was accelerated by a barrage of legislations. From January to December 1975, the government nationalized or took partial control of more than 100 companies, banks, large-scale agricultural farms, insurance and other financial institutions;

nationalized both rural and urban land; and proclaimed ceiling on private investment. It set up institutions (associations, cooperatives, unions) and organized both rural and urban communities into hierarchies.

The collectivist economic system of the Derg deliberately suppressed the market forces and instead geared all its efforts to strengthen the public sector. It designed discriminatory polices (both monetary and fiscal) aimed at benefiting the socialized and penalizing the private sector. The regime legally prohibited private economic activity (ownership) and discouraged entrepreneur ship; publicly owned all financial and productive institutions; adopted conservative fiscal management policies; and adopted a controlled price and wage, exchange rate, and financial and trade policies.

The banking system consisted three public banks and one insurance corporation despite the several public and private financial institutions previously. The National Bank of Ethiopia controlled and supervised all banks and financial institutions. Most of the banking services were concentrated in major urban areas and the productive sectors were not given priority. It also adopted restrictive policies that include limiting budget deficit and cutting back capital expenditure and others such as   price control, official over valuing of birr and a freeze wages of senior government staff to combat inflation and reduce deficits. The government controlled the cereal market and export of commodities; restricted land rental and wage labor; and imposed huge tax burden on rural households.

The socialist government developed, through the Office of the National Council for Central Planning (ONCCP), a series of annual and ten-year perspective development plans. These plans merely helped to handle some urgent economic problems, such as shortages of food and consumer goods, decline in productivity, lack of foreign exchange and rising unemployment but failed to attain long-term development objectives.

In general, the post revolution period can be viewed to have gone through four phases. Internal political upheaval, armed conflict, radical institutional reform, huge military budget and hence little economic growth (0.4 percent on average annually) marked the 1974-78 period. Moreover, the current account deficit and the overall fiscal deficit widened, and the retail price index jumped, growing at 14.9 percent, on average, annually (WB, 2006).

In the second phase (1978-80), the economy began to recover as the government consolidated power and implemented institutional reforms, that the security conditions improved as internal and external threats (the Ogaden war and rebel activity in Eritrea) subsided and as a result of the good weather. Consequently, GDP, agricultural production and manufacturing grew at average annual rates of 3 percent, 2 percent, and 11.3 percent respectively. The current account deficit and the overall fiscal deficit remained below 5 percent of GDP during this period (MoFED, 2004).

The economy experienced a setback in the third phase (1980-85). Four factors, the 1984-85 drought that affected almost all regions of the country and consumed scarce resources, the stagnation in the manufacturing sector as agricultural inputs declined, lack of foreign exchange and declining investment, and very large military establishment , accounted for such downturn.

Despite improvements in weather, the economy continued to stagnate during the last period (1985-90). The lingering effects of the 1984/85 drought undercut growth and contributed to the overall stagnation of the economy. During this period, the current account deficit and the overall fiscal deficit worsened to annual rates of 10.6 and 13.5 percent, respectively, and the debt service ratio continued to climb.

Examining overall economic performance during the whole period, it is evident from table 4.2 that output growth on average declined to 2 percent (the per capita GDP growth being -0.7 percent). Likewise, Growth in agriculture, industry and services sectors decelerated to 1.6 percent, 1.4 percent and close to 3 percent respectively. Growth in the industrial sector was as a result of expansion in the electricity and water works while expansion in the services sector was due to growth in public administration and defense (6.4 percent), education and domestic and other services. Unlike the imperial regime, the role of large and medium scale manufacturing, construction, transport and communication and real estate greatly declined during this régime.

At the end of this period Ethiopia had a gross domestic product of 10.9 billion birr (in 180/81 prices) and a per capita income of about 222.5 birr one of the lowest per capita incomes of any country in the world. The current account and overall deficit widened approximating 2 percent and 0.3 percent of GDP and the consumer price index went up to 10 percent signaling a soar in average prices.

Table 4.2 macroeconomic indicators

Indicator	Average 1974/75-1990/91		Average 1974/75-1990/91	
Real GDP growth		sector	Share in cap exp	Share in total exp
GDP per cap growth	-0.7	Economic devpt	88.9	31
Total	1.9	Social service	9.4	16.7
Agriculture	1.6	General service	1.7	52.3
Industry	1.4	Capital	-	29.9
Services	2.95	indicator	In millions	% share to GDP
CPI	9.9	Currnt Accn defici	(-)588.7	1.93
		Overall balance	(-)71.6	0.237

Source: own calculations based on data from MoFED for GDP and expenditure; and NBE for current account and overall balances.

Such down ward growth trend could be partly associated to the neglect of development activities. Close to 53 percent of the annual budget was committed to general government services. Defense expenditure accounted for 33 percent of government expenditure. Current expenditures as share of GDP grew from 13.2 percent in 1974/75 to 26.1 percent in 1987/88 largely due to rise in expenditures on defense and general services. Social and economic services together received 47 percent of the total spending lower than that of the imperial period.

In total, abrupt political change, drought, unstable political climate and huge defense budget, inflexible government policy, land tenure difficulties and land fragmentation and lack of confidence by the private sector; and the overall low level of technology seriously affected the economy. Falling productivity, soaring inflation, growing dependence on foreign aid and loans, high unemployment, and a deteriorating balance of payments all combined to create a deepening economic crisis.

On March 5, 1990, president Mengistu officially declared the failure of the Marxist economic system and announced the adoption of a new strategy for the country's future progress and development, in which he proposed decentralization in planning, free market and mixed economy. Despite the several additional reforms that included allowing unlimited participation of the private sector in certain areas of the economy; restructuring agricultural and farm price policies (1988); stopping continues land reform restriction on labor wage; and finally abandoning the Marxist economic system (1990), the economy failed to improve.

However, deteriorating economic structure, discontent of people towards the regime, strong resistance from rebel forces across the country (increasingly taking ethnic form) and external economic strangulation increased. Thus, the plan proved irrelevant in view of the deteriorating political and military situation that led to the fall of the regime in 1991.

4.1.3 The Post 1991 Period (EPRDF regime)

This period begins in 1991 next to the fall of the military regime and the ascent to power of the EPRDF. The return to relative peace after 1991 provided an opportunity for recovery to the Ethiopian economy that was in deep crisis by the beginning of 1990s. The new government adopted economic reforms, initiated in 1988 by the Dergue government as a 'mixed economy' option to the command economy, that took on the form of structural adjustment programs (liberalization) with the support of the Bretton Wood institutions (IMF and WB). Liberalizing agricultural market, price liberalization, a large devaluation, tax reforms and some steps towards liberalizing international trade included some of the early measures of the liberalization policy.

Reforms focused more on financial market liberalization, privatization, developing an investment code, government finance framework, fertilizer market reforms, initiatives regarding input and extension delivery and further international trade liberalization in the late 1990s. In addition, Sectoral policies included plans related to education, roads, health and agricultural extension, mainly involving substantial donor -financed capital expenditure. According to Dercon (2000) the increased spending on these sectors involved higher GDP share to capital expenditure and more importantly seemed to have more poverty concern than the previous ones.

The economic performance of the Ethiopian economy in the first decade of the EPRDF rule has been remarkable. First, there was smooth transition to peace and market oriented economy along with broad macroeconomic stability. Despite a large devaluation and domestic price liberalization, inflation was generally within one digit during this period. Fiscal deficit was also kept within reasonable limits. Secondly, there has been notable growth in GDP at both sectoral and national level. The detail on the key macroeconomic indicators of the Ethiopian economy for the whole period and sub periods is provided in the tables below.

Table 4.3 Macroeconomic indicators by sub period

Indicator	Average, in birr		
	1991/92-2002/03	2003/04-2008/09	1991/92-2008/09
GDP per capita in 80/81 price	241	-	-
GDP per capita growth	0.9	6.3	2.7
Real GDP growth			
Total GDP	3.8	11.6	6.3
Agriculture	1.1	11.5	4.5
Industry	6.1	10.6	7.6
Services	6.7	13	9
Inflation (CPI)	4.28	-	-
Gross capital formation as a share of GDP (%)	18.8	24.1	20.5
Exports as a share of GDP (%)	10.4	16	12.2
Trade deficit as share of GDP	10.3	19	13.2
Current account balance(millions)	-3282	-33071	-13211.6
Overall balance of payments (millions)	39.6	-477.7	-132.8

Source: Author's computations based on data from MoFED for GDP; WB for CPI, exports, imports and trade deficit; and IMF for Gross fixed capital formation.

Table 4.4 reveals that real GDP growth between 1990/91 and 2002/03 averaged 3.8 percent per annum and this figure rises to 5.4 percent if we limit the period to 1992/03 to 2000/01. Growth was the highest in the services sector (6.7 percent on average per annum) followed by industry (6.1 percent annual average). The agricultural sector grew at 1.1 percent on average per year and its share to GDP has declined to 45 percent by the end of the decade. Growth in output was large enough to bring about net improvements of 0.9 percent in the average income of the people. Over the same period, although it peaked in the transition period, inflation generally remained relatively low averaging 4.28 percent per annum. Dercon (2001), citing (IMF, 1999) writes that exchange rate has also retained a certain degree of stability with the spread between the official and parallel market exchange rate narrowing to only about 2 percent.

Exports of goods and services as share of GDP reached 10.4 percent of GDP on average per year showing a recovery from the very low levels during the transition period. Coffee export accounted for 60 percent of the total export earning and the coffee boom during the mid 1990s contributed to the revival. Non-coffee exports remained relatively low. On the other hand, imports as a share of GDP approximated 20.7 percent exceeding exports by around two to one resulting in a deficit of the difference in the balance of trade. Gross fixed investment also increased to an average annual share to GDP of 18.8 percent from about 10 percent in the early 1990s. The share of private investment in total gross investment is still about 60 percent, similar to levels in the late 1980s. Exports and gross investment figures suggest that a more structural change has occurred with more out ward oriented economy and a picking up investment.

Fiscal policy became relatively prudent. The average fiscal deficit as a share to GDP declined to 6 percent much lower than that above 10 percent in the early 1990s largely obtained via a collapse in government expenditure in the transition period (19.2 percent) and a recovery of government revenue from the mid-1990s. Moreover, close 35 percent of the government budget was spent on capital projects and expenditure on general services declined to only 45 percent while economic and social services could jointly attract more than half of the total budget. Defense spending fell to as low as 19.6 percent.

Table 4.4 Fiscal and Monetary indicators

Indicator	Period Average		
	1991/92-2002/03	2003/04-2008/09	1991/92-2008/09
Government revenue (% to GDP)	13.2	15.8	14.7
Government expenditure (% to GDP)	19.2	24.5	21.
Fiscal deficit (% to GDP)	6	11.3	6.3
Government expenditure on:			
Economic services (% to total)	29.8	38.9	34.4
Social services (% to total)	24.9	31.8	27.8
General services(% to total)Capital	45.3	24.3	33.7
expenditure (% to total)	34.9	49.2	42.6
Defense expenditure (% to total)	19.6	9.6	14.2

Source: own calculation based on data obtained from MoFED

The war between Eritrea and Ethiopia disrupted this evolution that defense expenditure rose to about 10 percent of GDP in 1999 and 2000 weakening the fiscal stance and leading to cuts in capital expenditure to social sectors and large increases in domestic financing of the fiscal deficit.

However, Dercon (2000) argues that the overall performance does not look impressive compared with the situation in the early 1980s. According to him much of the growth has been a recovery from the low GDP per capita levels in the early 1990s and inflation, expenditure and deficit were not very different from the levels in the 1990s.

Turning to the second period, economic activity has been generally strong when measured in various metrics. According to government statistics, the economy registered a consecutive six-year double digit GDP growth of above11 percent. The growth was not just higher but more broad-based and less volatile with all of the three main economic sectors growing not below 6 percent and more than 60 percent of the national income statistics categories growing 8 percent or more compared to only 30 percent in the previous six years (Access capital, 2009). Improved yields and rising land use in agriculture and rapid growth in government spending and private sector services in services sector were key drivers of growth.

Exports grew at annual average rate of 25 percent (with 13 percent average volume) which is about 3/2 times world export growth implying a rise in Ethiopia's market share. The export mix is now more diversified with coffee exports down to 36 percent from 60 percent a decade ago and oilseeds, pulses, flowers, chat, leather products and gold becoming more important. Almost all of the Ethiopia's exports are undertaken by the private sector. Foreign direct investment was up by five folds in the last six years. Total government debt has been reduced to moderate levels (36 percent of GDP) due to large scale debt relief by international lenders down from 100 percent of GDP in 2001. The external debt service burden is now less than one fifth of what it was in start of the decade. As a result, government spending on public goods notably in health, education, roads, electricity and telecommunications expanded.

However, these significant economic improvements remain modest when evaluated in per capita terms, relative to the size of the economy (GDP), compared to Africa's leading performers, the evolutionary progress in small scale agriculture and some monetary policy failures. Measures such as GDP per capita, export per capita and others do show some gains but also a very low base. For instance, although Ethiopia's per capita GDP rose from $450 (in ppp) in 1990 to $1055 in 2007, it remains 10 percent of the average world per capita income ($9543). Despite large nominal increases in some economic indicators, progress is low relative to the overall size of the economy (share to GDP). The cumulative growth since 1992 is in the mid single digits and is just below what was achieved by the three African success stories (Mozambique, Uganda and Tanzania).

4.2 Sources of Growth: Model Estimates

We have in the preceding sections reviewed the theoretical and empirical literature relevant to the study; and examined the political economy milieu for growth and the performance of the Ethiopian economy during the different regimes over the last five decades. It is now worth examining the quantifiable contribution of the various components of the growth process.

In particular, this section presents and discusses the estimates for the contributions of labor and capital inputs, and total factor productivity (TFP) to aggregate output growth for the period 1961-2009 using econometric model-based growth accounting exercise. To this end, first the unit root stationarity and cointegration tests results are examined. The overall regression results and mainly the growth elasticity estimates of the long and short run Cobb-Douglas production functions, specified in equations 3.8 and 3.9 in the methodology part, are subsequently investigated. Next, the growth accounting exercise estimates of the contribution of factor inputs and total factor productivity, using the output elasticity estimates and the actual growth rates in output and factor inputs, for the three different regimes have been thoroughly discussed. Finally, an attempt is made to compare the findings of the current study to that of earlier similar studies.

4.2.1 Estimation of the CD production function

Estimation of production functions involves times series variables, such as output, capital and labor inputs that may follow a time trend. There is then a need to test the relevant variables for stationarity to safeguard against the possibility of a spurious regression before proceeding with estimation. Estimating an equation through ordinary least squares (OLS) technique using non-stationary variables overstates the usual t-ratios making them unreliable for testing the statistical significance of the relationship between variables. Hence, the Dickey and Fuller (DF) unit root test has been chiefly used to check the stationarity properties of the variables. The correlogram test is also used in addition. The detailed unit root (DF or ADF) test result for each variable is presented in tables A1 and A2 in appendix A. But the test values for the first difference of the logarithm of output, labor and capital inputs is presented in table 4.5 below for ease of reference. As revealed in appendix A, the logarithms of output, labor and capital inputs, and rainfall at level were found to be non stationary with or without including a time trend. Nonetheless, the test values in table 4.5 below for the first differences of the logarithm of these variables provide evidence for stationary. Sated differently, the time series for the logarithm of each of these variables is integrated of order one (I_1).

Table 4.5 Test values for the stationarity of the first difference of logarithm of Y, L, and K

Variable	$D[\ln Y(-1)]$		$D[\ln K(-1)]$		$D[\ln L(-1)]$	
	r^*_c	r^*_{ct}	r^*_c	r^*_{ct}	r^*_c	r^*_{ct}
Coefficient	-0.74	-0.82	-1.24	-1.27	-1.30	-1.41
t-statistic	-5.06	-5.54	-8.65	-8.86	-9.20	-10.27
t- critical at 1 %	-3.6	-4.17	-3.58	-4.17	-3.57	-4.16
R^2, d-w stat	0.36,1.87	0.41,1.89	0.62,2.01	0.64,2.05	0.65,1.56	0.70,1.63

Sources: own estimates (using E-views 5)

Note: r_c and r_{ct} stand, respectively, for the existence of constant term, and trend and constant term in the regression.

Regression of the non stationary (at level) variable of the logarithm of output on the other non stationary variables may be feared to produce a nonsense regression. However, if these variables are found to be cointegrated, the same regression would be meaningful. All the variables are found to integrated of the same order (I_1) and cointegration test can be reasonably carried out. The Dickey-Fuller (DF) and the cointegrating regression Durbin-Watson (CRDW) tests are performed to check if the variables are cointegrated or not. The DF test examines the stationary of the residual from the cointegrating regression. The results of both tests are reported in appendix A of table A1. The test results of the DF test indicates that the computed τ – value (τ =-2.21) is larger in absolute value than the 5 percent critical τ – value (τ_c =-1.94) suggesting that the regression of logarithm of output on the logarithm of the other variables can be non-spuriously carried out. In the same way, the cointegration regression Durbin Watson value obtained in the cointegration regression ($dw = 0.56$) is greater than the 10 percent critical value of ($dwc = 0.51$) again reflecting cointegration.

Having made the required diagnostic tests, the time series data on output, and labor and capital inputs has now become valid for estimation. The Cobb-Douglas production function specified in equation 3.8 and reproduced in 4.1 below is chosen for estimation and analysis.

$$\ln Y_t = \beta_0 + \beta_1 \lambda + \beta_2 \ln K_t + \beta_3 \ln L_t + \varepsilon_t \qquad (4.1)$$

Where Y_t, K_t and L_t represent output and capital and labor inputs at time t. While β_2, β_3 and β_1 stand for, respectively, the output elasticities of capital and labor inputs, and total factor productivity growth, ε_t refers to the random error term.

The choice of production function specification between CD form and CES form is based on the test of the nested hypothesis in equation 3.4 The CES production function is preferred provided the parameter for the term $(\ln k - \ln l)^2$ in that equation suffices statistical significance; the CD form otherwise. The estimation of both production functions is reported in appendix-A of table A3 and the CES estimated regression model is replicated in equation 4.2 below. The coefficient for the fifth term in equation 4.10 below ($\beta_4 = 0.0188$) is found to be statistically insignificant at all levels of significances with t-statistics value of 0.64. Thus, the term that justifies the significance of the CES form in the nested hypothesis vanishes. This suggests the relevance of the CD production function to model the growth process. It is worth noting that the use of trans-log production has been ruled out due to the lack of data on proxies for technological advancement and the problems of multi-collinearity associated to it.

$$\ln Y = 6.86 + 0.002t + 0.15 \ln K + 0.75 \ln L + 0.0188 (\ln K - \ln L)^2 \qquad (4.2)$$

Accordingly, two versions (short run and long run) of the CD production function have been estimated using the Ordinary Least Squares (OLS) method. The cointegration test result in appendix-A of table A2 justifies the estimation of the error correction model. Cointegration implies the relationship between variables to be expressed as ECM just like equation 3.9 in chapter three. The details of the OLS estimates of both the short and long run CD production functions taking data from 1961-2009 are presented in table 4.6 below.

Table 4.6: Estimation results of the long and short run CD production functions (1961-2009)

Regressors	Long run model dependent variable: $\ln Y$ number of observations=49			Short run model dependent variable: $\Delta \ln Y$ number of observations=48		
	Coefficient	t-statistics	std.error	Coefficient	t-statistics	std.error
Constant	6.22	1.258	4.941	0.017	1.464	0.011
Time	0.001	0.160	0.008			
$\ln K$	0.305	4.498*	0.068			
$\ln L$	0.617	1.681**	0.367			
$\Delta(\ln K)$				0.072	1.43	0.05
$\Delta(\ln L)$				0.60	1.94**	0.32
U_{t-1}				-0.17	-1.81**	0.09
R^2, DW, LL	0.97, 0.56, 57.2, Prob>F=0.00			0.17, 1.55, 81.5		

Source: own estimates

Note: *significant at 1 % percent level

    **significant at 10 percent level

However, before proceeding with analyzing the results of the estimation, additional diagnostic tests for the overall significance of the regressions are undertaken for both models. The histogram-normality test indicates that the residuals from both models follow standard normal distribution (with probabilities of 0.22 and 0.14 each). The white hetroschedaticity test for the Error correction model reveals the non existence of the problem (with probability of 0.66 percent). Likewise, the Breush-Godfrey serial correlations LM test accepts the null hypothesis that there has not been serial correlation between the residuals in the error correction model (with a probability of 0.07 percent). The Breusch-pagan test for hetroschedasticty ensures that the variance is time invariant (with a probability of 0.19 percent) in the long run model. The partial correlation plot in the test for correlogram of the squared residuals seems that of the white noise error. The reports for these tests is given in appendix-A of table A4. These tests corroborate the test results of the basic unit root and cointegration tests conducted above.

The above table gives a summary of the estimated results for the two versions of the CD production function specified, respectively, in equations 4.5 and 4.6. The estimates for the long run version of the model are presented in the first three columns of the table. The coefficient for the logarithm of capital ($\ln K$) is found to be highly statistically significant at 1 percent level of significance with a long run growth elasticity value of 0.31. This implies that a one percent average growth in the productive stock of capital on average contributed 0.31 percentage points to economic growth over the reference period. Similarly, the output elasticity coefficient for the logarithm of labor input ($\ln L$) is statistically significant at 10 percent significance level indicating that an average one percent growth in employment increased output by 0.61 average percentage points during the same period.

Moreover, the sum of the growth elasticity coefficients for labor and capital inputs (that is 0.91) differs from unity supporting the assumption of variable returns to scale made in specifying the CD production function in the proceeding section. The coefficient on the time variable has a value of 0.001 and is not statistically significant at all levels of significance. It means that no meaningful progress in technology was registered on average during the study period.

Likewise, the regression results of the Error correction model are reported in the next columns of table 4.6. Despite the significant growth elasticity of capital in the long run, the coefficient for capital ($\Delta \ln K$) is statistically insignificant in the short run. This finding complies with fact that capital investments often involve gradual returns. Increased stock of capital in any particular year may not result in an immediate improvement in output level.

On the other hand, the coefficient for labor ($\Delta \ln L$) was found to be statistically significant at 10 percent level of significance with growth potency of 0.62. Change in labor accounted for a large part of the short run fluctuation in output growth. This seems natural because it is relatively easy to bring people directly through the production process and expect an immediate return. The adjustment coefficient value of -0.17 is found to be statistically significant at 10 percent level of significance. This suggests that only 17 percent of the deviation from the equilibrium output in the previous period is being made up in the current period.

4.2.2 Growth Accounting for Ethiopia

The growth elasticities of labor and capital inputs based on estimation of the two version Cobb-Douglas production function are presented and analyzed in the preceding sub-section. Growth elasticities measure only percentage contributions to output growth of a one percent change in factor inputs. The contribution of overall changes in factor inputs and total factor productivity to actual output growth however depends on the joint effect of growth rate of factor inputs and the respective output elasticities. Hence, the actual change in output is split in to the shares of its components with the help of growth accounting exercise defined below.

$$\frac{\Delta Y}{Y} = \beta_1 + 0.30 \frac{\Delta K}{K} + 0.61 \frac{\Delta L}{L} \qquad (4.3)$$

Where 0.30 and 0.61 are partial output elasticities reported in table 4.6. The terms $\Delta Y/Y, \Delta K/K$ and $\Delta L/L$ measure the actual growth rates in output, and capital and labor inputs during the reference period. Multiplication of the partial output elasticities by the compound input growth rates yields share of each input to growth of the economy and the total factor productivity growth parameter β_1 (Solow residual) is estimated as a residual from the same equation the results of which are given in table 4.8.

Table 4.7: Trends in growth of output, and capital and labor inputs

Sub period	Average growth rate		
	Output	Capital	Labor
1961-67	4.26	7.66	2.51
1968-74	3.18	5.75	2.18
1975-81	1.88	3.68	2.13
1982-90	2.48	6.69	2.12
1991-96	3.64	7.32	2.26
1997-03	3.76	8.11	2.72
2004-09	11.49	15.97	4.42
1961-09	4.18	7.84	2.36
Growth elasticities	Labor=0.61 and capital=0.30		

Source: own computations based on MoFED and UN data and model estimates above

The trend in the growth of aggregate output and capital and labor inputs for the entire study period as well as the sub periods is given in table 4.7 in the preceding page.

Given the estimated growth elasticities and the actual growth in GDP and factor inputs, the growth accounting exercise has been carried out for the whole period and for other seven sub-periods each containing six to nine years. The period and sub period averages for growth in output and labor and capital inputs are worked out to undertake the growth decomposition. Years in each period are chosen as much as possible in a way that it belongs to one of the three different regimes.

Table 4.8: growth accounting for Ethiopia (1961-2009): time series based model

| Period | Output growth | Sources of growth | | |
		capital	labor	TFPG
Long run model				
1961-1967	4.26	2.30	1.56	0.40
1968-1974	3.18	1.72	1.35	0.11
1975-1981	1.88	1.10	1.32	-0.54
1982-1990	2.48	2.01	1.31	-0.84
1991-1996	3.64	2.20	1.40	0.04
1997-2003	3.74	2.43	1.68	-0.36
2004-2009	11.49	4.79	2.74	3.96
1961-2009	4.18	2.36	1.62	0.40
short run model				
1961-1967	4.26	0.13	1.53	2.60
1968-1974	3.18	0.10	1.33	1.76
1975-1981	1.88	0.06	1.30	0.52
1982-1990	2.48	0.11	1.30	1.08
1991-1996	3.64	0.12	1.38	2.13
1997-2003	3.74	0.14	1.66	1.96
2004-2009	11.49	0.27	2.70	8.53
1961-2009	4.18	0.13	1.60	2.65

Source: own computation based on the MoFED data for growth in output and factor inputs.

This makes analysis of the growth process across different policy regimes possible. The growth accounting exercise is performed for both the long run and the short run (ECM) versions of the model under the three (the imperial, the Derg and the EPRDF) different regimes. The results of the growth accounting exercise are reported in table 4.8.

4.2.2.1   The Imperial Period

Table 4.8 presents the sources of growth in Ethiopia for different periods of the three regimes in the last five decades. For the imperial government, only the last fourteen years of rule for which data is available are included in the growth accounting exercise. During the first-seven year sub period GDP grew at an average rate of 4.26 percent. The contribution of the average expansion in the stock of productive capital over the same period is estimated at 2.3 percent. This figure accounts for 54 percent of the output growth for that period. The share of growth in labor employment to economic growth averaged 1.56 percent which is 37 percent of the output growth. Total factor productivity growth however contributed only 0.4 percent which is equivalent to 9.3 percent of the overall growth.

Hence, change in capital input accounted for a good part of the positive output growth registered during 1961-1967. This can be partly explained by the large government investment in infrastructure and social services under the two development plans. In addition, the then free market economic policy created conducive environment for private economic activity that the longstanding landed gentry started to transform into emerging entrepreneur class by investing in large scale farms and food-processing firms. The average share of investment in GDP reached 16.6 percent which is greater than the average for the entire imperial period (14 percent of GDP).

In the second sub period, the economy grew on average at about 3.2 percent. Growth in capital input contributed 1.72 percent to GDP growth while the share of labor averaged 1.35 percent. The share of the overall improvement in productivity declined to 0.11 percent. Capital explains most of growth record during this period despite the decline in economic performance (particularly during the last three years) as a result of drought and political instability.

When we look at the entire imperial period, economic growth averaged 3.72 percent. Capital takes close to 2 percent of the growth in GDP while labor accounts for 1.5 percent and the remaining balance (0.27 percent) goes to improvement in factor productivity. Growth during this period is thus largely explained by capital accumulation. This partly relates to the large public capital investment in transport, communications, construction works and social services. There was also increased private investment in capital-intensive farms, food processing industries, and financial institutions. The contribution of labor has also been encouraging with its share averaging 38 percent of the change in output. In conclusion, the positive growth performance during the last fourteen years of the imperial rule is largely explained by factor accumulation and the role of total factor productivity was negligible.

4.2.2.2   The Derg Period

Passing to the Derg regime, GDP growth averaged 1.88 percent while the share of capital and labor to output growth ,respectively, amounted 1.10 percent and 1.32 percent during the first period. The total factor productivity growth was -0.54 percent. The contributions of physical capital and total factor efficiency exhibited sharp declines while labor exhibited relatively low changes.

This period is characterized by internal political upheaval, radical institutional reform and huge military spending. The sudden political change, the subsequent internal unrest, the war against external invasion (war with Somalia) and the hard control policy of the Derg disrupted economic activity. The disruption in the operation of productive economic agents interrupted capital formation and thus lower capital role to growth. In the same way, the large military investment (misallocation of productive resources), repressive policies and rain fed nature of agriculture could explain negativity of total factor productivity. Economic growth and contribution of factor inputs and factor efficiency however slightly improved in the late years as a result of implementation of institutional reforms, better security conditions and good weather.

The economy in the second period grew at a rate of 2.48 percent. Capital and labor inputs, and total factor efficiency contributed 2.01 percent, 1.31 percent and -0.84 percent to output growth. Seemingly, the share of capital and labor to output growth increased. However, the fact that the combined effect greatly exceeds the overall growth indicates a massive decline in productivity. Such slow down in factor efficiency is attributed to the 1984 drought that affected almost all regions of the country and consumed scarce resources, instability, restrictive policies and huge military investment that persisted during this period.

Taken as a whole, growth decelerated to close to 2.2 percent during the military regime. Total factor productivity on average declined at -0.69 percent. This and the superficially high contribution of physical capital to output growth reflects the extent to which capital accumulation was exaggerated by going to non-productive uses and hence was not 'true' capital accumulation. In addition, unstable political climate, regulatory policy of the Derg and recurring drought had adverse impact on factor efficiency. This is substantiated by Alemayehu et al (2005) in which he finds that negative factor efficiency is related to weather and external shocks.

4.2.2.3   The EPRDF Period

The sources of growth during this period can be analyzed in two major sub-periods; the period beginning from the coming to power of the regime to 2003 and the recent special growth period (2004-09). This is meant to examine the sources of recent fast growth records independently.

To begin with, GDP growth in the first sub period averaged 3.69 percent where capital and labor inputs, respectively, contributed 2.31 percent and 1.54 percent and total factor productivity on average declined by -0.16. The rise in the stock of physical capital explained much of the growth in output even after allowances for productivity declines. The role of increased employment was also the next important source of GDP growth during this period.

Much of the output growth during this period came from the services (5.2 percent) and industrial (4.1 percent) sectors while the role of agriculture was minimal (1.3 percent). Large and medium scale manufacturing, construction, and electricity and water works generated much of the growth in industrial sector while growth in services sector was dominated by expansion of education, health, communication and transport services. Growth in these subsectors was in turn driven by increased public and private investment as a result of the revival in external finance and policy reform initiated by the new government. Dercon (2000) emphasizes the increased share of capital expenditure on education, health and road construction to GDP during this period. The share of investment in GDP thus rose to about 17 percent. This supports the finding that physical capital had strong contribution to economic growth over the first 13 years of the EPRDF rule.

At least two evident factors can be mentioned for the negativity of factor efficiency between 1991 and 2003, particularly the last seven years. Growth in agriculture during this sub period highly fluctuated with the highest (14.7 percent) being in 1996 and the lowest (-12.6 percent) in

2003 reflecting its dependence on weather shocks. Likewise, the war with Eritrea (1998-2000) had adverse economic consequences. Compared to the pre war period, capital expenditure went down by about 2 percent of GDP and fiscal deficit increased by more than 3 percent of GDP. Even worse, private borrowing amounted 4.1 percent of GDP in 2000 (Dercon, 2000). Such declines in public investment and possible crowd out of private investment could lead to productivity slowdown.

The second period (2004-09) witnessed a different feature about the growth process in general and mainly the sources of that growth. GDP growth averaged 11.4 percent rare in the economic history of Ethiopia and the highest among a handful of non oil producing countries of Africa and worldwide. Physical capital contributed 4.79 percent to GDP growth while the share of labor and total factor productivity, respectively, averaged 2.74 percent and 3.96 percent. Most of the output growth (42 percent), like the previous ones, is attributed to physical capital accumulation closely followed by rise in factor efficiency (34 percent). Although in total the contribution of factor accumulation dominates (66 percent), the share of productivity gain was exceptionally sizeable during this period.

Growth during this period has been more broad-based with the main economic sectors strongly growing at above six percent. Agriculture grew on average at 10.7 percent while industrial and services sectors grew at 10 percent and 12.95 percent respectively (MoFEd, 2009). Expansion in the dominant agriculture sector was driven by rising land use and improved yield. Expansion in public infrastructure and social services together with rapid growth in private service sector growth –retail trade, hotels, transportation, financial services and real estate-were key drivers of growth in service sector. Construction and large and medium manufacturing constituted much of the growth in industrial sector (MoFED, 2009). Foreign direct investment was up more than five folds and the share of investment to GDP averaged 23.78 percent (Access capital, 2009). The massive public capital investment in infrastructure and social and health services, expanded foreign and domestic private investment in large and medium scale manufacturing, construction and real sate suggest for the large role of capital to economic growth.

In theory, a rage of variables such as macroeconomic stability, openness of the economy, financial sector development, investment to GDP ratio, budget deficit, government consumption, foreign debt and etc influence total factor productivity in an economy(Ahmed, 2007). In addition,

Rahel (2003), citing Senhadji (1999), writes the role of favorable initial conditions and terms of trade, political stability , lower external debt and public consumption to be associated with higher levels of TFP growth. Weather shocks are also important in rain fed agriculture.

Ethiopia experienced major macroeconomic imbalances –high inflation, weak revenue base, private sector credit crowd out and shortage of foreign exchange-during the last couple of years. In contrast, according to a review by Access Capital (2009), external debts drastically declined to 12 percent of GDP from a peak of 100 percent of GDP in 2001 while the ratio of investment to GDP rose to close to 24 percent from 17 percent in earlier years. Besides, the ratio of sum of imports and exports to GDP, a measure of openness, according to WDI data for 2009 has increased. Budget deficit declined to 4.3 percent of GDP from beyond 7 percent in previous periods (MoFED, 2009). The same sources indicate that the last six years has seen an average 20 percent deposit growth, 40 percent profit growth, improved service and lower overhead costs by Ethiopian banks giving a clue of the development in the financial sector. Finally, the volatility of growth due to dominance of rain fed agriculture has been greatly reduced and agricultural production was relatively stable.

The positive and strong contribution of factor efficiency can be explained by, despite imbalances, the facts that the economy was more open; the share of investment to GDP rose; external debt greatly declined; budget deficit improved; and reduced shocks from weather.

Now that source of output growth during each regime is discussed, it is plausible to extend it to the entire study period. The economy on average grew at 4.18 percent .Physical capital and labor, respectively, contributed 2.4 percent and 1.6 percent while total factor productivity shared only 0.19 percent of growth in GDP. Hence, physical capital accumulation was the dominant sources of output growth (57 percent of 4.18 percent) followed by labor (38 percent) while the role of factor productivity was insignificant (4.5 percent). Growth in Ethiopia in the last five decades is thus explained by factor accumulation. Summary of the sources of growth for the entire sample period is given in figure 4.1 below.

The high share of investment to GDP during the imperial and the EPRDF regimes chiefly stemming from massive public and private investment, respectively, in infrastructure and social and health services; and large scale farms, manufacturing and financial institutions in the former and considerably expanded government expenditure in alike sectors and the spurred private investment (foreign and domestic) in real estate, transportation, manufacturing, construction and financial services in the later are likely sources of the strength of the share of capital investment during the study period.

The age old rain-fed nature of agriculture, devastative wars against foreign aggression, prolonged political unrest, restrictive economic policy and vulnerability to shocks might have jointly deterred productivity during the study period despite the revival in the recent growth period (2004-09) due to substantial decline in the impact of these factors and productivity gains from improvements in other areas.

Figure 4.1: Overall and sub period sources of GDP growth

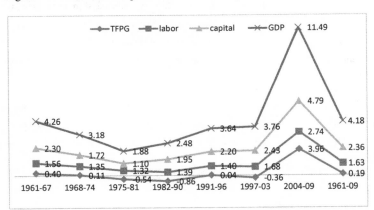

Source: estimations above

Note: GDP= growth rate in GDP; capital=share of capital to growth; labor =share of labor to growth; and TFP=share of factor efficiency to growth

4.2.3 Comparison to Earlier Studies

The empirical findings of this paper need to be contrasted to the existing empirical work on sources of growth in Ethiopia (or sub Saharan Africa) to understand its deviations or similarities.

The literature on Ethiopia's long run growth process is limited. Comprehensive empirical studies about the growth process can be found in the works of Easterly (2006), Alemayehu et al (2005), Netsanet (1997), Alemayehu et al (2007), Alemayehu et al (2008), Dercon (2000). These researchers utilized different approaches and obtained varying results about the sources of growth in Ethiopia for different sample periods.

William Easterly in his work "Growth in Ethiopia: retrospect and prospect: employed the methodology of Klenow-Rodriguez-Clare 1997 , that relate growth to capital deepening beyond which capital growth exceeds output growth to decompose the sources of growth between 1951 and 2001. He splits growth between capital deepening and total factor productivity and finds that factor productivity explained 0.59 percent of the 0.68 percent growth per person while capital accounted for only 0.08 percent. Although direct comparison is difficult, both studies found that the contribution of factor productivity was highly negative during the military regime.

Alemayehu and Befekadu (2005) used the Collins and Bosworth bench mark estimation to determine the sources of growth between 1960 and 1997. They decompose growth per person in to the share of capital per worker, education per worker and residual using 0.35 and 0.65 as output elasticities of capital and labor respectively. The results of their growth accounting exercise indicate that capital plays a dominant role in defining the growth record while total factor productivity remained negative over the sample period. The contribution of education per worker was weak.

The findings with regard to capital and total factor productivity can be directly compared. Both the study by these authors and the present study, though with different approaches, obtained the identical results that the share of capital and TFP is generally positive in both the imperial and the current regime. TFP overall was negligible due to the high decline in productivity in the Derg regime despite high superficial capital share.

Another study by Alemayehu et al (2008) used both micro and macro level data to estimate the Cobb-Douglas production function for the period 1953-193 (Ethiopian fiscal year). The macro version discovered the importance of labor in driving growth while TFP is generally positive. The micro version in contrast finds the dominant role of land and reduced roles of labor. The sharp contrast in the share of labor and capital to growth, to these authors, emanates from the

65

neglect of 'land' as a regressor. Even though with different sample periods, the results obtained in these studies contradict with what is obtained by this study perhaps different data sets has been used.

Source of growth exercise based on an endogenous growth-like model whose parameters are derived from cross country regression by Alemayehu Geda (2008) finds the higher contribution of base variables (such as initial income/endowment, life expectancy, age dependency ratio, terms of trade shocks, etc). In addition, this study emphasizes the strong role of physical capital in explaining economic growth in Ethiopia.

Finally, growth accounting exercise conducted by Tahari et al (2004) based on a literature on production function estimates for developing countries (the output elasticity of capital being 0.3) found that growth in sub Saharan Africa was driven by factor accumulation while the contribution of TFP was nil between 1960 and 2002. Furthermore, capital and labor accounted for 18 and 1.5 percent of to the average growth of 3.2 percent consistent to this papers finding.

CHAPTER-FIVE

CONCLUSION AND RECOMMENDATION

5.1. Conclusions

The research work presents the estimation of the sources of growth in the country. The empirical analysis was undertaken based on econometric model-based growth accounting exercise using data for the period 1961-2009. Accordingly, the main research findings are summarized as follows:

Estimation of the CD production function indicated that both labor and capital has been important in determining the long run growth process. Although the output elasticity of labor is found to be stronger (with growth elasticity of 0.61), the growth elasticity of capital (0.31) has also been statistically significant. In contrast, only labor is found to be crucial in explaining the short run growth process with growth potency of 0.60. The output elasticity of capital is found be both very small and statistically insignificant in the short run.

The growth accounting exercise which shows the complete picture of the growth process reveals that physical capital has been the dominant sources of economic growth in Ethiopia for the last five decades. Growth in capital on average explained more than half of the growth in output between 1961 and 2009. The contribution of capital is the highest in the imperial and the current regimes where massive productive investment by public (in infrastructure and social services) and private sectors has been undertaken. Capital accumulation during the Derg time contributed very low to output growth suggesting the extent to which capital was diverted to non productive activities.

Labor has been the second most important component of the growth process. It has on average accounted for 38 percent of the output growth during the reference period. The share of labor did not change much except for slight slow down during the Derg regime until it substantially increased over the EPRDF regime perhaps due to the priority given to agriculture and labor intensive small and micro enterprises. The contribution of total factor productivity has been generally negligible with growth share of only 4.5 percent over the same period. It remained positive during the imperial regime while it was highly negative during the Derg likely

67

associated to the unstable political climate, regulatory policy of the government and recurrent drought (particularly the 1985) in that period. Exceptionally, the share of increased productivity to growth mounted to as high as 34 percent during the 2004-09 period. The facts that the economy has been more open; external debt significantly went down, budget deficit improved; investment share to GDP rose; and reduced shocks to agricultural production might have contributed to such spur in productivity.

Existing empirical studies on the sources of growth in Ethiopia utilized different approaches and came up with varying results. The findings of this study are found to be consistent with, despite the different approaches used, what was obtained by Alemayehu et al (2005) and Alemayehu (2008). Both emphasized the role of physical capital in explaining the positive growth record. In the same way, studies on the sources of growth in sub Saharan Africa such as Tahari et al (2004) and Bosworth and Collins (2003) obtained similar results.

5.2. Recommendations

Based on the empirical findings about the sources of growth in Ethiopia concluded in the preceding section, the afore-mentioned policy recommendations can be legitimately proposed.

- The source of growth analysis points to the paramount importance of physical capital to output growth. This has often taken the form of massive public investment in infrastructure and social services. Hence, investment in infrastructure such as energy, communication, transport, and education and health are found to have growth payoffs and the government should thus continue investing on such public goods.

- While the contribution of labor is found to be encouraging, its marginal productivity is particularly strong implying more returns from labor intensive production techniques and more payoffs to investments on labor. Labor using technologies are also in line with the poverty alleviation priories of the country. Thus, efforts to exploit labor consuming means of production and investments to augment the quality of labor (education and training) should be strengthened.

- The role of the service sector has been increasing while industry did not change much like other poor income countries' economies. Hence, it is imperative to encourage investment in the industrial sector given the lesson that investment in physical capital contributed to much of the growth in output in the past decades

- Finally, highly negative total factor productivity was recorded during the Derg when there was command economic system, unstable political climate and weak productive investment while Positive TFP was registered during the imperial and the EPRDF regimes that pursued free market economic systems; undertook more productive investments; and managed relative peace and stability reflecting more returns from increased investment, peace and freed markets.

REFERENCES

Ahmed, Khalil. "Source of Growth and Total Factor Productivity: A case study of Pakistan", University of Punjab, 2007.

Antras ,pol . contributions to Macroeconoics' ,Harvard University, 2004

Baneshwor, Purano. "Nepal: Country Study Report", Institute for Integrated Development Studies (IIDS), 2002.

Barro, J. "Determinants of Economic Growth: A cross-country empirical study", National Bureau of Economic Research, Cambridge, 1998.

Bosworth, Barry, Collins. "The Empirics of Growth: An Update", Brookings Institution and Georgetown University,2003.

Central Statistical Agency, "Summary and statistical report of the 2007 population and housing census: population size by age and sex", Addis Ababa, 2008.

Dercon, Stefan. "Growth and Poverty in Ethiopia in the 1990s: an economic perspective", Center for the Study of African Economies, Oxford University, 2002.

Devereux, Stephen, Sharp, Kay. "Is poverty really falling in rural Ethiopia?", Institute of Development Studies , University of Sussex,2003.

Easterly, William. "Growth in Ethiopia: retrospect and prospect," center for global development, institute for international economics, 2002.

Economic commission for Africa, "Ethiopia-Good policies, Decent outcomes: Tracking performance and progress,"2002.

Geda ,Alemayohu, Befekadu Degfe. "Explaining African Economic Growth Performance", African Economic Research Consortium, 2005.

Geda, Alemayehu, Shimeles, Abebe, weeks, John. "The pattern of growth, poverty and inequality in Ethiopia: which way for a pro- poor growth?", university of London, 2008.

Geda, Alemayehu. "The political economy of growth in Ethiopia", Cambridge African Economic History Series, 2008.

Greiner, Alfred, Semmler, Willi, Gong, Gang. "The Forces of Economic Growth", Princeton University Press, 2005.

Gujarati, N."Basic Econometrics" McGraw-Hill companies, fourth edition, 2004.

Jesus, Felipe. "A Decade of Debate about the Sources of Growth in East Asia: How much do We Know about Why some Countries Grow Faster than others", Asian development bank, 2006.

Lau, J, Park, Jungsoo. "The Sources of East Asian economic growth revisited", Stanford University and the State University of New York, 2003.

Ministry of Finance and Economic Development (MOFED). Ethiopia: Sustainable Development and Poverty Reduction Programme, 2002.

Petrakos, George, Arvanitidis, Paschalis. "Determinants of economic growth: The experts' view", University of Thessaly, 2001.

Petrakos, George, Arvanitidis, Paschalis , Pavleas ,Sotiris. "Determinants of economic growth: The experts' view", University of Thessaly, 2007.

Rahel, kasahun. "Ethiopian recent growth performance: A survey of the literature", Addis Ababa, 20003.

Romer, David. "Advanced Macroeconomics: Empirical applications", Third edition, McGraw-hill, 2006.

Snowdon ,Brian. "The Enduring Elixir of Economic Growth", Harvard University, 2006.

Tahari Amor, Ghura ,Dhaneshwar, Akitoby ,Bernardin, Brou ,Emmanuel. "Sources of growth in sub Saharan Africa",IMF,2004.

The African Development Bank Group Chief Economist Complex, "Ethiopia's Economic growth Performance: Current Situation and Challenges", vol.1, issue15, 2010.

UNDP, "Human Development Report: Beyond scarcity: Power, poverty and the global water crisis, New York, 2006.

UNDP, "Human Development Report: Overcoming barriers: Human mobility and development", New York, 2009.

Wang, Haifeng, Lawson, Colin. "Growth Accounting Versus Regression in a Cross-country TFP exercise", university of Bath, 2004.

APPENDICES

Appendix A: Diagnostic tests

Unit Root Tests (DF and ADF)

Table A1: Unit root test for logarithms of output, labor, capital and rainfall: At level

| Variable | Estimate | | | | | |
| | With time trend | | | without time trend | | |
	t-statistics	t-critical	coefficient	t-statistics	t-critical	coefficient
$\ln Y(-1)$	0.54 -	-4.16	-0.04			
$\ln K(-1)$	-1.25 -	-4.16	-0.09			
$\ln L(-1)$	-0.77 -	-3.18	-0.05			
$\ln R(-1)$	-2.52 -	-2.89	-0.24			
$U_t(-1)$				-2.21	-1.95	-0.24

Note: Reject the null the hypotheses of unit root if t-statistics > t-critical; all the coefficients above are statistically significant at 1 percent but the lagged error term is significant at 5 percent

Table A2: Unit root test for the first difference of logarithms of output, labor, capital and rainfall:

| Variable | Estimate | | | | | |
| | Without time trend | | | with time trend | | |
	t-statistics	t-critical	coefficient	t-statistics	t-critical	coefficient
$D[\ln Y](-1)$	-4.93	-3.58	-0.92	-5.68	-4.17	-1.08
$D[\ln K](-1)$	-5.20	-3.58	-1.24	-5.54	-4.17	-1.35
$D[\ln L(-1)]$	-6.06	-3.58	-1.2	-10.78	-4.17	-1.67
$D[\ln R](-1)$	-5.98	-3.58	-1.18	-5.87	-3.77	-0.86

Note: Reject the null the hypotheses of unit root if t-statistics > t-critical; all the coefficients above are statistically significant at 1 percent

73

Estimation Results

Table A3: Regression results for CD and CES production functions

Variable	Estimate				
CD, long run	Coefficient	t-statistics	t-critical	Standard error	$R^2.LL, dw,$
c	6.220	1.258	1.67	4.941	F=553
trend	0.001	0.160	1.67	0.008	
ln k	0.305*	4.497	2.61	0.067	0.97,57.2,0.56,
ln L	0.617**	1.681	1.67	0.367	
CD, ECM					prob>F=0.00
c	0.017	1.465	1.67	0.012	
D ln k	0.072	1.429	1.67	0.051	
D ln L	0.620**	1.935	1.67	0.321	0.174,81.5,1.54
u_{t-1}	-0.173**	-1.81	1.67	0.096	
CES					
c	6.857	1.352	1.67	5.072	
trend	0.002	0.212	1.67	0.008	
ln k	0.146	0.563	1.67	0.259	0.9, 57.4, 0.6
ln L	0.759	1.762	1.67	0.431	
$(\ln K - \ln l)^2$	0.019^	0.641	1.67	0.029	

Note:*=significant at 1 percent level;**=significant at 10 percent level; ^=insignificant at all

Table A4: Other Diagnostic Tests

Tests	probability	
	Long run	ECM
Histogram normality test	0.14	0.22
White hetroschedasticity test	-	0.66
Breush-Godfrey LM test	-	0.07
Breusch -pagan hetroschedasticity test	0.19	-

Appendix B

Estimation B1: Capital Stock Estimation

The capital stock has been estimated using the perpetual inventory method that relates the present stock of capital to accumulation of past streams of investment taken from Ahmed (2007).

$$k_t = w_t I_t + w_{t-1} I_{t-1} + ...w_{t-t} I_{t-t} \qquad 0 < w_{t-1} < 1 \qquad \text{A4.1}$$

Assuming geometric decay of capital stock and denoting the rate of depreciation by δ :

$$k_t = I_t + (1-\delta)I_{t-1} + (1-\delta)^2 I_{t-2} + ... (1-\delta)^t I_{T-t} \qquad \text{A4.2}$$

Writing A4.2 for I_{t-1} ; multiplying on both sides by $(1-\delta)$; and subtracting the resulting equation from A4.2 yields

$$k_t - (1-\delta)k_{t-1} = I_t \implies k_t = (1-\delta)k_{t-1} + I_t \qquad \text{A4.3}$$

The initial stock of capital is estimated by running a linear regression of logarithm of investment (GFCF) against the time trend as used by Ahmed, citing Nehru and Dhareshwar (1993). The estimated regression using gross fixed capital formation data for the sample period is:

$$\ln K = 20.3 + 0.039t \qquad \text{A4.4}$$
$$(t = 12.1) \quad (std.eror = 0.003) \quad R^2 = 0.7$$

Exponentiation of the constant term in A4.4 gives the initial investment of (654,904,512.2 birr) and the initial stock of capital can be computed using A4.5 given depreciation and output growth.

$$k_t = \frac{I_t}{\delta + g} \qquad \text{A4.5}$$

A depreciation rate of 6 percent suggested by Tahari et al (2004) for Sub Saharan Africa is used.